DRAMA CLASSICS

The Drama Classics series aims to offer the world's greatest plays in affordable paperback editions for students, actors and theatregoers. The hallmarks of the series are accessible introductions, uncluttered and uncut texts and an overall theatrical perspective.

Given that readers may be encountering a particular play for the first time, the introduction seeks to fill in the theatrical/historical background and to outline the chief themes rather than concentrate on interpretational and textual analysis. Similarly the play-texts themselves are free of footnotes and other interpolations: instead there is an end-glossary of 'difficult' words and phrases.

The texts of the English-language plays in the series have been prepared taking full account of all existing scholarship. The foreign language plays have been newly translated into a modern English that is both actable and accurate: many of the translators regularly have their work staged professionally.

Under the editorship of Kenneth McLeish, the Drama Classics series is building into a first-class library of dramatic literature representing the best of world theatre.

Series editor: Kenneth McLeish

Associate editors:
Professor Trevor R. Griffiths, *School of Literary and Media Studies, University of North London*
Simon Trussler, *Reader in Drama, Goldsmiths' College, University of London*

DRAMA CLASSICS *the first hundred*

The publishers welcome suggestions for further titles

DRAMA CLASSICS

THE BEAUX STRATAGEM

by
George Farquhar

edited and introduced by
Simon Trussler

NICK HERN BOOKS
London

A Drama Classic

This edition of *The Beaux Stratagem* first published in Great Britain as a paperback original in 1995 by Nick Hern Books Limited, 14 Larden Road, London W3 7ST

Copyright in the introduction © 1995 Nick Hern Books Ltd

Copyright in this edition of the text © 1995 Simon Trussler

Typeset by Country Setting, Woodchurch, Kent TN26 3TB
Printed by Seagull Books, Calcutta, India

A CIP catalogue record for this book is available from the British Library

ISBN 1 85459 154 1

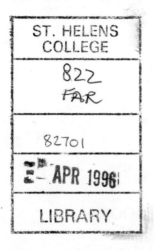

Introduction

George Farquhar (*c.* 1677-1707)

George Farquhar was born in Londonderry in northern Ireland,
probably in 1677, and would have been verging on adolescence
when the recently deposed James II besieged that city in 1689. His
father, as an Anglican clergyman, was a prime target for plunder,
and died soon afterwards, while the barely teenage George is said
to have fought (on King William's victorious side) in the subsequent
Battle of the Boyne in 1690 – which imposed the protestant succession (and a great deal of continuing grief) upon the Catholic majority
in Ireland.

Prematurely experienced in both the sorrows and the heroisms of
war, Farquhar proceeded from the local grammar school to Trinity
College, Dublin, in 1694, then in quick succession fell in love with
the theatre, performed at the Smock Alley playhouse in Dublin, gave
up acting after accidentally killing a fellow-performer in a stage duel,
and, like his lifelong friend and compatriot Robert Wilks, determined
on a future in London. Here, Farquhar's first comedy, *Love and a
Bottle,* was performed in 1698: but his precocious success as a playwright (discussed in more detail in the section 'The Comic Worlds of
George Farquhar', on p. vii) was interrupted by the renewal of war
with France in 1702. In 1704 he was granted a commission as a
Lieutenant of Grenadiers and sent off on a recruiting campaign to
the Midlands.

Meanwhile, in 1703, Farquhar had married, less from love than in
expectations of an income from his wife's fortune, which proved to
be non-existent. Indeed, he very soon found himself needing to
provide for their two daughters as well – at a time when he was
beginning to feel the effects of the wasting illness which we now
suppose to have been tuberculosis. He drew on his provincial
experiences in both of his last two plays, *The Recruiting Officer* and

The Beaux Stratagem (as also on his unhappy marriage in the last), but his rapidly declining health prevented him from building on their success, and he died in poverty in late May 1707. His friend Wilks paid for his funeral.

The Beaux Stratagem: What Happens in the Play

A pair of presentable but impoverished London gentlemen arrive at a Lichfield inn, plotting to repair their broken fortunes. One, Aimwell, pretends to be a lord (like his brother) to improve his chances of marrying a rich woman, while the other, Archer, has agreed to act as his servant – on condition that any dowry they secure is equally shared. After some dalliance with the bucolic landlord and his pretty daughter, Cherry, Aimwell sets his sights on Dorinda, the well-endowed daughter of Lady Bountiful – whose son, Squire Sullen, finds himself ill-matched with a spouse of great beauty but no inclination to share his hunting-and-drinking life-style. And so, while his 'master' woos the beauteous but innocent Dorinda, Archer makes illicit advances to the more knowing but cautiously receptive Mrs Sullen.

With Sullen safely out of the way, in quest of drinking companions at the inn, Archer inveigles himself into the household to pursue his amorous quest – on the very night chosen by a local band of highwaymen to rob the supposedly unprotected women. Aimwell, summoned by an anxious Cherry, helps to vanquish the intruders. He is renewing his suit to Dorinda when Sullen returns, in the company of his wife's brother, Sir Charles Freeman, who is determined to rescue her from her unhappy marriage. Freeman also brings news that Aimwell's brother has died – so Aimwell, now a lord indeed, can legitimise his love for Dorinda, which has by now grown to be real rather than self-serving. Sir Charles persuades the Squire into a divorce by consent – assisted by Archer's acquisition from the thieves of all the papers which give Sullen title to his wife's fortune.

This climax is open to all sorts of literal-minded criticism, not only for the coincidences that make it possible (a frequent enough convenience in this kind of comedy), but for the happy-go-lucky way in which Freeman pronounces a divorce for which the harsh legal constraints of the time gave no grounds. Indeed, *The Beaux Stratagem*, for all its social and psychological realism, treads a stylistic tightrope between such wish-fulfilment and the harsher realities of marriage – as it does also between the 'mannered' characters whose love-lives interweave in its main plot and the 'humours' characters whose economic needs and ambitions drive the action at a lower level. Among these latter are to be found the innkeeper Bonniface and his daughter Cherry, the highwaymen with whom Bonniface is complicit (Gibbet, Hounslow and Bagshot), and Sullen's all-purpose servant Scrub. There is also a pair of comic foreigners – Count Bellair, a captured French officer with whom Mrs Sullen has been platonically flirting, and Foigard, an Irishman who is treacherously serving as chaplain to the French prisoners. Such a presence in the neighbourhood was, of course, a reminder of the events beyond the play which had earlier made recruiting so topical a theme. But it is no less typical here than of Farquhar's earlier play-worlds that the tensions between actuality and artifice should generate dramatic energy rather than confusion.

The Comic Worlds of George Farquhar

The work of George Farquhar fits awkwardly into that over-extended category which critics have labelled 'Restoration comedy'. After all, Charles II had been 'restored' (following his father's execution and the 'interregnum' under Cromwell) in 1660, and the honeymoon he had enjoyed with his subjects was well over by 1677, the probable year of Farquhar's birth. Shortly afterwards, the crisis caused by the increasing probability that the Catholic James would succeed his brother to the throne set in motion the struggle for constitutional monarchy – a struggle which eventually led to King James's deposition during the 'bloodless revolution' of 1688-89, and the enthronement of William and Mary. The bourgeois sensibility of this royal couple proved well-suited to the changing national mood, as pursuit of the pleasure principle (so marked a feature of Charles II's reign) gave way before the sterner demands of the protestant work ethic.

It's true that Farquhar's near contemporaries Congreve and Vanbrugh (who both outlived him by some twenty years) continued to develop a dramatic tradition – of high-style, high-life 'comedy of manners', rooted in sexual dalliance – begun during the Restoration proper by Dryden, Etherege, Wycherley and Aphra Behn. But both Congreve and Vanbrugh gave up writing for the theatre soon after Jeremy Collier's influential anti-theatrical polemic, *A Short View of the Immorality and Profaneness of the English Stage*, published in 1698, had decisively articulated the changed temper of the times. Of the dramatists who have survived in the modern repertoire, Farquhar alone, it seems, found a spiritual as well as a chronological home in the society and the theatre of the years surrounding the turn of the seventeenth and eighteenth centuries.

Even so, he was barely twenty when he wrote his first play, *Love and a Bottle*, and could not at first afford (or perhaps did not yet know how to manage) so wholly personal a dramatic mode. It was not till his second play, *The Constant Couple*, of 1699, that he wrote a comedy in which conventional sexual pursuits were driven in part by new imperatives of cash and class – and the play found a responsive audience, proving the success of the season. But Farquhar evidently rested a little too long on the income and the laurels it brought him: and when, after eighteen months, he came up with a sequel, *Sir Harry Wildair*, the play suffered, as do so many of its kind, from the law of diminishing returns – though it managed a respectable first run, presumably on the strength of public curiosity to see how all the familiar characters would make out after marriage.

Farquhar's next play, *The Inconstant*, which took over and simplified the plot of John Fletcher's late Jacobean comedy *The Wild Goose Chase*, survived to its sixth night; but the death of King William in March 1702 eclipsed both the play's and Farquhar's own fortunes, and he set to work quickly on *The Twin-Rivals*, which had its first night in December of the same year. Subsequent criticism has been largely shaped by the need to account for the play's initial failure – which, one suspects, was due not to its relatively high moral tone (now becoming acceptable, indeed expected) but to its formal daring, in portraying unalleviated vice as a proper subject for realistic representation in comedy.

For Farquhar, the play is also very tightly plotted – around a younger brother's attempt to defraud his marginally older twin out of his inheritance. Sex here not only comes an acknowledged second to money, but is rather more closely connected with childbirth than theatrical convention usually acknowledged. There is more dramatic interest in the fraudulent lordling's demonstration of his unworthiness than in his eventual exposure, and although the play has not quite caught the tone of voice in which to be 'seriously funny', it does strike out in the new direction which Farquhar was shortly to follow through in *The Recruiting Officer* and *The Beaux Stratagem*.

In between, the short farce *The Stage-Coach* – dealing with the 'mistakes of a night', as true love blossoms in the attempt to save a girl from her guardian's preferred suitor – also anticipated Farquhar's last two plays, in its country setting of an inn. As Eric Rothstein says, 'it makes one hungry for the work he did not do' between its production late in 1703 and 1706. On the other hand, it was no doubt precisely Farquhar's escape from the incestuous world of literary and theatrical London during these years that tempered his final plays with the hard edge of experience – his brief military career providing a background for *The Recruiting Officer*, and his own unfortunate marriage a deep-felt source for his portrayal of sexual incompatibility in *The Beaux Stratagem*.

In Farquhar's mature plays, *The Recruiting Officer* (1706) and *The Beaux Stratagem* (1707), he does not abandon 'mannered' comedy as such; instead he transplants it, setting the plays outside London and including characters of the middling-to-lower social orders. In the process, not only are old conventions and rivalries – between town and country, between courtly elegance and city greed – made redundant, but the characters gain a capacity for experiencing subtler nuances of pleasure, and (perhaps more significantly) also for experiencing real pain. The modern critic Robert Hume makes an apt distinction – between the 'hard' comedy of Congreve and Vanbrugh, as late exponents of the Restoration mode, and the 'humane' school which, (along with Collier's censure) soon provoked both writers into abandoning playwriting. In the work of Farquhar alone do we find the broader sympathies of the new mode combined with the wit and verve of the old.

In the Shrewsbury setting of *The Recruiting Officer*, Captain Plume (the officer of the title) renews acquaintance with Justice Balance and his daughter Silvia – a pro-active lady, who not only inverts expectations by setting out in amorous pursuit of the negligent visitor, but puts on male breeches to advance her cause. Thanks to her brother's timely death, an inheritance soon gives a hard economic edge to her attractions; and the casual grief and offhand mourning of both father and sister (far more concerned with the dynastic than the emotional consequences of bereavement) make explicit a lack of family feeling which in earlier Restoration comedies is usually an unstated 'given'. No less clearly, for that matter, do we see the ready complicity of Justice Balance and his kind in the confidence tricks of the recruiting trade, as Plume and the faithfully duplicitous Sergeant Kite variously turn the heads and twist the arms of the local cannon-fodder.

Farquhar, of course, was here writing from personal knowledge – and whether or not this accounts for the mixture of amused nostalgia and contempt with which he appears to view the goings-on, it creates an interesting and energising balance of sympathies for an audience. Until well into our own century, however, both *The Recruiting Officer* and *The Beaux Stratagem* tended to be viewed rather as Restoration comedies *manqué*, and in revival rougher edges would be apologetic-ally honed, creative tensions resolved rather than dramatically sustained. Ironically, it took a foreigner, Bertolt Brecht, to recognise the sterner stuff of which *The Recruiting Officer* was made, in his own updated version, entitled *Drums and Trumpets*: and the English director Bill Gaskill acknowledged this Brechtian influence when, in his National Theatre productions of the nineteen sixties, he worked not to transplant fashionable metropolitan society into the provinces, but to relish and reveal the sharper local colours and broader social spectrum Farquhar brought to these last plays.

Mannered Comedy and the Married State

As the social historian Lawrence Stone has suggested, one side-effect of the Reformation was the displacement of the Catholic ideal of chastity and virginity by a belief in marriage as a state to be preferred and sanctified – 'holy matrimony' indeed. Moreover, with the protestant stripping away of all intermediaries between the individual and his or her God came the 'domestication' of a patriarchal authority that had previously lain with the parish and its priest: for the husband now found himself translated into a minister of the fireside, leading 'family prayers' in households described in 1644 by the puritan writer John Stalham as 'like so many little churches'.

In preference to the alliances of economic and dynastic convenience which had been the norm for those of any social standing in the sixteenth century, the puritans argued that the proper bases for a marriage were affection and compatibility. But given that authority over a woman passed from father to husband upon marriage, how could a dutiful daughter continue to obey her father if that meant accepting his choice of a husband she found repulsive? After himself making a disastrous marriage, the poet John Milton advocated in *The Doctrine and Discipline of Divorce* (1643) that divorce on the grounds of incompatibility should be made possible – going so far as to suggest that 'natural hatred' was 'a greater evil in marriage than the accident of adultery'. However, this freedom was to be reserved for husbands, not extended to wives: for, as he asked, 'who can be ignorant that woman was created for man, and not man for woman?' (Threatened with prosecution for unlicensed printing of his pamphlet, Milton proceeded to write, in *Areopagitica*, a resounding but ultimately no more disinterested polemic in favour of the freedom of the press.)

In spite of Milton, divorce on the grounds of incompatibility was not to be permitted for another three centuries – and such few divorces as *were* allowed remained socially scandalous, legally complicated, and prohibitively expensive. With the Restoration, moreover, the puritan belief in affectionate marriage lost credibility along with the cause of puritanism itself – so while Charles I's marriage with Henrietta Maria had seemed a very embodiment of the ideal of holy matrimony, his licentious son Charles II legitimised, so to say, adultery as the expected norm. And since the laws of inheritance required a wife to remain faithful (lest doubt be cast on the legitimacy of her offspring), the operation of a sexual double standard in high society became institutionalised. However, the general rule of Restoration comedy was that illicit sexual pursuit was rather more thrilling than its consummation – a rule apparently affirmed by no less an authority than the contemporary philosopher of the pleasure principle, Thomas Hobbes. Marriage, for four acts of a play, was merely an invitation to be cuckolded: only in the fifth did it become the means by which fortunes might be mended, and the necessary closure of the plot effected.

Farquhar accepts the convention that a husband and wife yoked at the outset of a comedy are likely to be in a state of misery. But he takes their unhappiness seriously – and without going to the opposite extreme of indulging the sentimentalist's urge to moralise over weaknesses and faults. He creates in Aimwell and Archer a pair of 'heartless' Restoration rakes, but proceeds to show that although one is impervious to change, the other becomes responsive to circumstance and reciprocated feeling. Archer is from the first the more conventionally manipulative of the two, and remains in every sense his own man (indeed, his possible future with a divorced Mrs Sullen is a matter about which both remain significantly vague). But in the case of the more reflective (even sensitive) Aimwell, there is the slow-maturing of a relationship as 'real' as the boundaries of this kind of comedy permit, and a 'repentance' which, while somewhat sudden, is neither last-minute nor unprepared. As in *The Recruiting Officer*, the death of an elder brother is a matter of congratulation, not commiseration, and clears the way for a modified if not exactly reformed rake to marry a woman for whom he appears to have learned respect as well as love.

The women are distinguished conventionally enough, with the innocent but eager-to-learn Dorinda set against the hard-schooled Mrs Sullen. But they are given an independence and, indeed, a prominence which had largely been denied them during the Restoration, other than by Aphra Behn – though more recently acknowledged by Congreve. Of course, female sensibility in the latter's *The Way of the World* is largely presented as reactive (however wittily) to male expectations, and so to a degree it is here. But it would be unhistorical to deny Mrs Sullen the typological descent which is implicit in such remarks as 'pride is the life of a woman, and flattery is our daily bread'. And when (as here) Farquhar shows the women alone together – rather than bantering with their beaux – there is that slight shifting of sexual ground in the debate which

had earlier been detectable in his presentation of Silvia and the no
less sceptical 'lady of fortune', Melinda, in *The Recruiting Officer*.

'The couple parted' are, as Archer observes, as pleased as 'the couple
joined'. Through the intervention of the aptly-named Sir Charles
Freeman, Farquhar goes further than Milton in suggesting not only
that the incompatibility of the Sullens should be a sufficient ground
for their divorce, but that mutual agreement (rather than masculine
dictat) is sufficient to effect it: 'Consent is law enough to set you
free.' Although the Married Women's Property Acts of the late
nineteenth century were a little less historically distant than divorce
by consent, Farquhar's resolution of the economic complications
here was no less a legal impossibility at the time than the Sullens'
simple disavowal of their marriage. Yet in a comedy all things are
possible, and the boundaries of the play-world are no more stretched
by turning the laws of matrimony than the laws of probability on
their head.

The Humours of Provincial Life

Ben Jonson remained admired during the Restoration – more so
even than Shakespeare, on account of what critics called his greater
'regularity'. But 'comedy of humours', as he had labelled his own
distinctive comic style – its intention to laugh people out of their
excesses and affectations – was usually no more than window
dressing around the edges of Restoration plays. Those (largely minor)
characters targeted for unsocial 'humours' are as often as not the
self-delighted 'fops', of high profile and low intelligence. On the
other hand, ridiculing 'humours' characters from the bourgeois ranks
of the 'cits' becomes as much a matter of class warfare as of comic
correction – part of a political as much as of an artistic agenda.

For these are plays in which privilege is presumed as of right. The
servants, such as there are, tend to be collusive confidants of their
masters or mistresses rather than in any way to represent a world
beyond that of privilege, whether bought by high breeding or by
hard cash. But the below-stairs world in *The Beaux Stratagem* is given
far more than such passing prominence. The richness of its texture in

párt derives, as Peter Womack points out, from the way in which its lesser inhabitants not only assume a comic dignity which is all their own but also ironically employ the idiom of their 'betters' (among an inventory of verbal tricks which, for landlord Bonniface, even includes the humble catchphrase). The fact that Archer operates at both levels adds to the complexity – and it is notable that, of all the characters, it should be the perceptive Cherry who most fully penetrates his disguise. What may or may not happen between Archer and Cherry is left to our imagination (just as poor Cherry remains one of the play's loose-ends), but we have the precedent of Rose in *The Recruiting Officer* to suggest that being a 'country girl' no longer carries quite its earlier dramatic implication of sexual availability. However, no more than Shakespeare in *As You Like It* is Farquhar so advanced as seriously to contemplate a more permanent alliance across the boundaries of class.

Not that the 'humours' characters are confined by social inferiority – or invariably distinguished by anti-social behaviour. Lady Bountiful thus displays her comic excesses both amusingly and from the very best of intentions – even, one presumes, to the occasional benefit of her patients. And if Count Bellair remains resolutely functional – present only to display his 'funny foreign accent' – presumably this is on account of Farquhar's realisation that, thanks to the French wars, London audiences would readily applaud such cheap chauvinism. Much better observed (and integrated into the plotting) is Foigard's mix of stage Irishness and French staginess – and Bonniface, too, is an original, while his even-tempered associates are allowed a professional dignity (not least in their apprehension) which anticipates that of their fellow-highwaymen in Gay's 'Newgate pastoral', *The Beggar's Opera*, written a couple of decades later.

Farquhar's 'Lichfield pastoral' presents the countryside neither as idyllic nor as peopled by imbeciles. And his motley characters are motivated more by the busy pragmatisms of the everyday than by the tunnel-visioned prurience of their Restoration forebears – or, for that matter, by the self-preening purity of such later 'sentimental' heroes as Young Bevil in Sir Richard Steele's significantly-titled *The Conscious Lovers*. As the critic Robert Hume sums up: 'The sense of human nature which emerges is benevolently sceptical, neither cynical nor saccharine. Farquhar indulges himself and us in the possibility of virtue, but without blinding himself to reality.'

London Theatre after the Restoration

When play-acting returned to London with the Restoration, after being banned by the puritans since 1642, it was at first in improvised theatres, converted from 'real' (or 'royal') indoor tennis courts by the two courtier-dramatists, Thomas Killigrew and Sir William Davenant, to whom the King gave his royal patent. Killigrew's company, under the King's own patronage, was the first to move to a purpose-built playhouse, the Theatre Royal in Bridges Street, Drury Lane, in 1663, but in 1672 this theatre was destroyed by fire, and the company found a temporary home in the converted Lisle's Tennis Court in Lincoln's Inn Fields. This had just been abandoned by Davenant's old company, the Duke of York's, on the completion of their own new playhouse, situated in Dorset Garden, south of Fleet Street, beside the Thames and not far from the city wall. Tradition attributes its design to Sir Christopher Wren, who was certainly responsible for the new theatre in Drury Lane to which the King's Men returned in 1674, and which survived with only minor modifications until 1791.

Looking back nostalgically to the Restoration years in 1725, John Dennis remarked that 'They alter'd at once the whole face of the stage by introducing scenes and women'. This was not quite true: the court masques of the Jacobean and Caroline period had employed some elaborate scenery, and the open-air theatres of the Elizabethans had long been giving way to indoor 'private' theatres, with greater potential for technical effects. The difference now was that the proscenium arch formed a 'picture-frame' for the painted perspective scenery, changed by the wings-and-shutters system, which provided a formalized background to Restoration comedy and tragedy.

But it was *only* a background: the actors performed on the extensive apron stage in front of the proscenium, in a relationship with their audiences no less intimate and uncluttered than that of their fore-bears. Indeed, Restoration theatres, which seated from around five to eight hundred, were actually smaller than the Elizabethan public playhouses, and their audiences, although not drawn quite so exclusively from a courtly elite as has sometimes been suggested, certainly felt themselves to be part of a social as much as of a theatrical occasion.

Quite how that 'crossing of the boundary' between actor and character, so clearly felt in Restoration prologues and epilogues, affected the acting of the play itself is not certain. But the style would certainly have been presentational rather than realistic – at a time, confessedly, when rituals of 'presentation' were of great importance to everyday courtly behaviour as well. So, with directors unthought of, and playwrights far less involved in the practical business of mounting a play than were their Elizabethan counterparts, the influence of the dancing-master was probably strong in matters of movement and stage grouping, as were the rules of social etiquette in the presentation of aristocratic behaviour – behaviour which had even evolved a 'language' to be 'spoken' by the nuanced fluttering of a lady's fan.

With just two companies of less than thirty players apiece, acting was an exclusive though not prestigious profession, its members as well-known personally to many in the audience as their own acquaintances in the pit or boxes. And, although the patents stressed that the introduction of actresses was a matter of morality – to correct the abuse of men appearing 'in the habits of women' – the intimacy between these players and their audiences was not confined to closeness in the auditorium. It was probably inevitable that, in the absence of a traditional route for women into the profession, some actresses in a licentious age should have achieved their positions through sexual patronage – though it is also indisputable that Elizabeth Barry, for example, despite her path being smoothed by the notorious rake Lord Rochester, became a remarkable tragic actress, while Nell Gwyn, although she owed her early chances to being the mistress of Charles Hart, was already a striking comic actress before she caught the eye of the King.

In the aftermath of the alleged 'Popish Plot' of 1678, practical politics increasingly consumed the attention of the courtly audiences, and, with the theatre as yet holding little appeal for their social inferiors, the two companies joined forces in 1682. London's theatregoers were for thirteen years served by the Drury Lane company alone: then, in 1695, Thomas Betterton, the leading actor of his generation, took a group of players back to Lincoln's Inn, having quarrelled with the manager at Drury Lane, the overbearing and underpaying Christopher Rich. The 'warfare' which ensued between these two theatres was already in full swing when Farquhar's first play, *Love and a Bottle*, reached the stage in December 1698.

It might have seemed that Farquhar, in entrusting this play to Drury Lane, would be on the losing side, for Betterton had taken with him to Lincoln's Inn Fields the best-known players of the day, including the leading actresses Elizabeth Barry and Anne Bracegirdle – and the opening production there, of Congreve's *Love for Love*, set a sparkling standard. But Drury Lane – besides being a far superior theatre – enjoyed the advantages as well as the inexperience of youth, and by 1699, while all the great names at Lincoln's Inn were past or passing their prime, Drury Lane was attracting the luminaries of the new generation. Susannah Verbruggen, William Pinkethman, and the young Colley Cibber had remained loyal, and over the next few years William Bullock, Farquhar's friends Robert Wilks and Henry Norris, and his protégée Anne Oldfield all joined the company. As Cibber put it in his *Apology*, 'Betterton's people . . . were most of them too far advanc'd in years to mend; and tho' we, in Drury Lane, were too young to be excellent, we were not too old to be better'.

Cibber's own *Love's Last Shift* was the outstanding success in 1696 at Drury Lane, to be followed by Vanbrugh's comic sequel, *The Relapse*, in 1697 – while Farquhar's achievement of over fifty performances of *The Constant Couple* in the first season alone set the seal on the young company's slow but sure ascendancy. Farquhar remained loyal to Drury Lane until a number of its best actors, weary as much of Rich's manner as of his management, defected in the autumn of 1706 to Vanbrugh's new Queen's Theatre in the Haymarket, where Betterton's company had been in residence since its opening in the previous year. Farquhar contributed a prologue to the first production of the new season at the Queen's, in October 1706, and it was here that *The Beaux Stratagem* opened in the following March. In the event, this was to be one of the very few successes at a playhouse whose acoustics made it unsuitable for the spoken drama. By 1708, it was given over to opera, and the actors had returned to Drury Lane, where (after a few further vicissitudes) a new management, including Cibber and Wilks, at last inaugurated a period of relative stability – albeit also of artistic sterility.

The period of theatrical 'warfare' had almost exactly coincided with Farquhar's own brief theatrical career – and witnessed not only his own comedies, but all those of Vanbrugh, the greatest of Congreve's, and the most significant work of Cibber and Steele. The audience for them was, by comparison with Elizabethan times, still small, but its tastes and its social composition were changing – in ways which remain the inflammable stuff of critical debate, among both theatre and social historians. But one verifiable fact is, simply, that a new, much younger generation of actors was getting into its stride, in the work of an equally young generation of dramatists. Although Vanbrugh had just reached his thirties, Congreve and Farquhar were both in their early twenties when they first found theatrical success – and Wilks, when he played Farquhar's Sir Harry Wildair in 1699, was just half the age of Betterton, who was turning sixty when he had created the part of 'young' Valentine in Congreve's *Love for Love*.

It was Wilks who took the role of Archer in *The Beaux Stratagem* – and of the fourteen roles in that play no fewer than nine went to players with previous experience of Farquhar's work. The steady and stalwart John Mills, like Wilks a veteran of six Farquhar roles, was aptly cast as Aimwell. Colley Cibber, a late recruit to the defecting company, declined the offer of Scrub, electing instead to play Gibbet (an intriguing choice for one of nature's fops), thus enabling Dicky Norris to triumph in the role of the versatile manservant – as did his fellow-comedian, the bluff but dextrous William Bullock, in that of Bonniface. Mrs Bradshaw, although an actress new to Farquhar, proved a winning Dorinda, while Anne Oldfield matured from her Silvia in *The Recruiting Officer* to play Mrs Sullen (and a few weeks later also took on Lurewell, in an opportune revival of *The Constant Couple*). The play was an immediate success, and had passed its twelfth triumphant performance when, around 20 May 1707, its author died in a garret in St Martin's Lane.

A Note on the Text and Punctuation

The text of *The Beaux Stratagem* was, unusually, prepared for press prior to its first performance, presumably owing to Farquhar's illness, but none the less with his active assistance. Indeed, its publisher, Bernard Lintot, doubled the usual advance to a dramatist to £30, perhaps in recognition of the author's condition. The text of the first edition of 1707, on which the present edition is based, thus bears the distinctive authority of a dying author's attention to the last fruits of his genius.

In the interests of clarity and series style, certain conventions of eighteenth-century typography have been modernised in this edition: thus, the italicising of proper names and the surfeit of initial capitalisation have alike been silently modified. Spelling has been updated, except where an earlier form suggests a distinctive pronunciation or stress. Speech headings and the positioning of stage directions have also been regularised.

The original punctuation has, however, been retained. Our modern tendency to make punctuation accord with grammatical useage is a legacy of the later eighteenth-century desire for 'correctness', and reflects Latinate rules rather than what regulates pauses and emphases in the way people actually speak. It is possible that in this respect many old playscripts may reflect typographical as much as dramatic useage: but even the former will bear a closer relationship to contemporary habits of speaking than our modern tendency to 'hear' dramatic dialogue through the form it takes on a printed page – a habit which, as a little random eavesdropping will readily affirm, is not in the least reflective of the pace and pauses of colloquial speech. Farquhar's use of the dash, incidentally, might be compared to the modern playwright's stage direction for a 'beat': a very slight pause seems indicated, whether for a change of direction on the speaker's part, a moment's reaction on the listener's, or simply a rhetorical catching of the breath.

Simon Trussler

For Further Reading

Those few critical monographs on Farquhar which may be recommended to the general reader include A. J. Farmer's concise introductory pamphlet in the 'Writers and Their Work' series (London: Longmans, for the British Council, 1966) and Eric Rothstein's cogent, detailed study in the 'Twayne's English Authors' series (New York: Twayne, 1967). There is also a straightforward and readable (though occasionally over-conjectural) biography, *Young George Farquhar*, by Willard Connely (Cassell, 1949). Although not focused on our play, Max Stafford-Clark's *Letters to George: the Account of a Rehearsal* (London: Nick Hern Books, 1989) is an articulate and accessible record of one director's approach to *The Recruiting Officer*.

A sampling of shorter critical essays on the *The Recruiting Officer* and *The Beaux Stratagem* can be found in the Macmillan 'Casebook' series, edited by Raymond A. Anselment (1977), and there are introductions to *The Beaux Stratagem* in the modern editions which have appeared in the New Mermaid series (Benn, 1976) and the Regents Restoration Drama series (Arnold, 1977). Among more broadly-based works, J. L. Styan's *Restoration Comedy in Performance* (Cambridge, 1986) is recommended for its investigation of stage conventions, and Peter Holland's *The Ornament of Action* (Cambridge, 1979) for its discussion of the relationship between text and performance.

For the specialist reader, a new critical edition of Farquhar's *Works*, edited by Shirley Strum Kenny, was published in 1988 by Oxford University Press – the first since the two-volume *Complete Works* edited by Charles Stonehill (London: Nonesuch Press, 1930). The Mermaid selection edited by William Archer (London: Unwin, 1906), still widely available secondhand, includes *The Constant Couple* and *The Twin-Rivals* as well as *The Recruiting Officer* and *The Beaux Stratagem*. The single more advanced full-length critical study is Eugene N. James's *The Development of Farquhar as a Comic Dramatist* (The Hague: Mouton, 1972).

General works which deal more than tangentially with Farquhar tend to 'squeeze' him, either chronologically or into their own critical straitjacket. Bonamy Dobrée's *Restoration Comedy 1660-1720* (Oxford: Clarendon Press, 1924) is well-tempered, tolerant, and superficial. Robert D. Hume's *The Development of English Drama in the Late Seventeenth Century* (Oxford: Clarendon Press, 1976) is a far superior work, but although pertinently directed to the problems of our supposedly transitional period, it, too, is relatively neglectful of Farquhar. Other critical studies include Kenneth Muir's *The Comedy of Manners* (London, 1970), and Ben Ross Schneider's *The Ethos of Restoration Comedy* (Illinois University Press, 1971).

An otherwise valuable collection of essays, *Restoration Drama*, edited by John Loftis (Oxford University Press, 1966) symptomatically includes nothing on Farquhar, though it reprints L. C. Knights's influential attack on the drama of the period alongside a defence by F. W. Bateson. The standard work on the Collier controversy remains *Comedy and Conscience after the Restoration*, by Joseph Wood Krutch (New York: Columbia University Press, 1924), while John Loftis's *Comedy and Society from Congreve to Fielding* (Stanford University Press, 1959) is helpful on Farquhar as a 'topical' writer.

The fifth volume of *The Revels History of Drama in English* by John Loftis *et al.* (London: Methuen, 1976) covers the period 1660 to 1750, and does deal with the theatre as such are *The London Stage 1660-1700: a Critical Introduction*, by Emmett L. Avery and Arthur H. Scouten, and *The London Stage 1700-1729: a Critical Introduction*, by Avery alone (Carbondale: Southern Illinois University Press, 1968). Some of the essays in *The London Theatre World*, edited by Robert D. Hume (Carbondale: Southern Illinois University Press, 1980), are also helpful. Of the few books on acting and production styles, Jocelyn Powell's stimulating *Restoration Theatre Production* (London: Routledge, 1984) deals at length with Congreve – but, as is so often the case, scarcely at all with Farquhar. Illuminating and complementing all of these by reprinting a wide range of contemporary documentation and illustration is a volume in the 'Theatre in Europe: a Documentary History' series, *Restoration and Georgian England, 1660-1788*, edited by David Thomas (Cambridge University Press, 1989).

Farquhar: Key Dates

1677 *c*. Born in Londonderry.

1689 Presumably still in Londonderry during the Jacobite siege. Volunteered to fight in the Battle of the Boyne in 1690?

1694 Entered Trinity College, Dublin, as a 'sizar' – receiving scant board and tuition in return for menial duties.

1696 Left Trinity College without his degree, and acted at the Smock Alley Theatre in Dublin, making his debut as Othello.

1697 Left for London to try his fortune as a playwright.

1698 His first play, the comedy *Love and a Bottle* (published 1699), performed at Drury Lane in December, and his anecdotal novella, *Adventures of Covent-Garden*, published anonymously.

1699 First performance of *The Constant Couple; or, A Trip to the Jubilee* (published 1700) at Drury Lane in November.

1701 *Sir Harry Wildair* performed at Drury Lane in April.

1702 His adaptation of Fletcher's *The Wild Goose Chase* as *The Inconstant* (published 1702) and the satirical comedy *The Twin-Rivals* (published 1703) both performed at Drury Lane. His miscellany of verse and letters, *Love and Business*, published, including the epistolary 'Discourse upon Comedy'.

1703 Marriage to Margaret Pemell, a widow with three children, whose poverty apparently surprised him. The short farce *The Stage-Coach* (published 1704), adapted from the French, performed at Lincoln's Inn Fields in December, or January 1704.

1704 Commissioned as a Lieutenant of Grenadiers, securing him a small but reliable income of £54 a year. Received almost £100 from a Dublin benefit performance of *The Constant Couple*. Birth of his first daughter, Anne Marguerite.

1705 On recruiting service in Lichfield and Shrewsbury. Birth of his
      second daughter, Mary.

1706 *The Recruiting Officer* (set in Shrewsbury) performed successfully
      at Drury Lane in April and published. Well received, but
      Farquhar was already ill, presumably with tuberculosis, and
      may have sold his commission to raise money.

1707 *The Beaux Stratagem* (set in Lichfield) performed at the new
      theatre in the Haymarket in March, and published. But
      Farquhar now gravely ill, and, in his thirtieth year, he died in
      May in a 'back garret' in St. Martin's Lane.

Advertisement

The reader may find some faults in this play, which my illness prevented the amending of, but there is great amends made in the representation, which cannot be match'd, no more than the friendly and indefatigable care of Mr. Wilks, to whom I chiefly owe the success of the play.

GEORGE FARQUHAR

Prologue

Spoken by Mr. Wilks.

When strife disturbs or sloth corrupts an age,
Keen satire is the business of the stage.
When the Plain-Dealer *writ, he lash'd those crimes*
Which then infested most – the modish times:
But now, when faction sleeps and sloth is fled,
And all our youth in active fields are bred;
When thro Great Britain's fair extensive round,
The trumps of fame the notes of Union sound;
When Anna's sceptre points the laws their course,
And her example gives her precepts force:
There scarce is room for satire, all our lays
Must be, or songs of triumph, or of praise:
But as in grounds best cultivated, tares
And poppies rise among the golden ears;
Our products so, fit for the field or school,
Must mix with Nature's favourite plant – a fool:
A weed that has to twenty summers ran,
Shoots up in stalk, and vegetates to man.
Simpling our author goes from field to field,
And culls such fools, as may diversion yield;
And, thanks to Nature, there's no want of those,
For rain, or shine, the thriving coxcomb grows.
Follies, to night we show, ne'er lash'd before,
Yet, such as Nature shows you every hour;
Nor can the pictures give a just offence,
For fools are made for jests to men of sense.

Dramatis Personae

Men

AIMWELL	{ Two gentlemen of broken fortunes, the
ARCHER	first as master, and the second as servant
COUNT BELLÀIR	A French officer, prisoner at Lichfield
SULLEN	A country blockhead, brutal to his wife
FREEMAN	A gentleman from London
FOIGARD	A priest, chaplain to the French officers
GIBBET	A highwayman
HOUNSLOW	{ His companions
BAGSHOT	
BONNIFACE	Landlord of the inn
SCRUB	Servant to Mr. Sullen

Women

LADY BOUNTIFUL	An old civil country gentlewoman, that cures all her neighbours of all distempers, and foolishly fond of her son Sullen
DORINDA	Lady Bountiful's daughter
MRS. SULLEN	Her daughter-in-law
GIPSEY	Maid to the ladies
CHERRY	The landlord's daughter in the inn

Scene, Lichfield

Act I

Scene, an inn. Enter BONNIFACE *running.*

BONNIFACE. Chamberlain, maid, Cherry, daughter Cherry, all asleep, all dead?

Enter CHERRY *running.*

CHERRY. Here, here, why d'ye bawl so, Father? d'ye think we have no ears?

BONNIFACE. You deserve to have none, you young minx; – the company of the Warrington coach has stood in the hall this hour, and no body to show them to their chambers.

CHERRY. And let 'em wait farther; there's neither red coat in the coach, nor footman behind it.

BONNIFACE. But they threaten to go to another inn tonight.

CHERRY. That they dare not, for fear the coachman should overturn them tomorrow. – Coming, coming: here's the London coach arriv'd.

Enter several people with trunks, band-boxes, and other luggage, and cross the stage.

BONNIFACE. Welcome, ladies.

CHERRY. Very welcome, gentlemen – chamberlain, show the Lion and the Rose.

Exit with the company.

Enter AIMWELL *in riding habit,* ARCHER *as footman carrying a portmantle.*

BONNIFACE. This way, this way, gentlemen.

AIMWELL. Set down the things, go to the stable, and see my horses well rubb'd.

ARCHER. I shall, sir.

Exit.

AIMWELL. You're my landlord, I suppose?

BONNIFACE. Yes, sir, I'm old Will. Bonniface, pretty well known upon this road, as the saying is.

AIMWELL. O Mr. Bonniface, your servant.

BONNIFACE. O sir – what will your honour please to drink, as the saying is?

AIMWELL. I have heard your town of Lichfield much fam'd for ale, I think I'll taste that.

BONNIFACE. Sir, I have now in my cellar ten tun of the best ale in Staffordshire; 'tis smooth as oil, sweet as milk, clear as amber, and strong as brandy; and will be just fourteen year old the fifth day of next March old style.

AIMWELL. You're very exact, I find, in the age of your ale.

BONNIFACE. As punctual, sir, as I am in the age of my children: I'll show you such ale – here, tapster, broach Number 1706 as the saying is; – Sir, you shall taste my *Anno Domini*; – I have liv'd in Lichfield man and boy above eight and fifty years, and I believe have not consum'd eight and fifty ounces of meat.

AIMWELL. At a meal, you mean, if one may guess your sense by your bulk.

BONNIFACE. Not in my life, sir, I have fed purely upon ale; I have eat my ale, drank my ale, and I always sleep upon ale.

Enter TAPSTER *with a bottle and glass.*

Now, sir, you shall see. (*Filling it out.*) Your worship's health; ha! delicious, delicious, – fancy it burgundy, only fancy it, and 'tis worth ten shilling a quart.

AIMWELL (*drinks*). 'Tis confounded strong.

BONNIFACE. Strong! It must be so, or how should we be strong that drink it?

AIMWELL. And have you liv'd so long upon this ale, landlord?

BONNIFACE. Eight and fifty years upon my credit, sir; but it kill'd my wife, poor woman, as the saying is.

AIMWELL. How came that to pass?

BONNIFACE. I don't know how, sir; she would not let the ale take its natural course, sir, she was for qualifying it every now and then with a dram, as the saying is; and an honest gentleman that came this way from Ireland, made her a present of a dozen bottles of usquebaugh – But the poor woman was never well after: but howe'er, I was obliged to the gentleman, you know.

AIMWELL. Why, was it the usquebaugh that kill'd her?

BONNIFACE. My Lady Bountiful said so, – She, good lady, did what could be done, she cured her of three tympanies, but the fourth carried her off; but she's happy, and I'm contented, as the saying is.

CHERRY. Who's that Lady Bountiful, you mention'd?

BONNIFACE. Od's my life, sir, we'll drink her health. (*Drinks*.) My Lady Bountiful is one of the best of women: her last husband Sir Charles Bountiful left her worth a thousand pound a year; and I believe she lays out one half on't in charitable uses for the good of her neighbours; she cures rheumatisms, ruptures, and broken shins in men, green sickness, obstructions, and fits of the mother in women; – the kings-evil, chin-cough, and chilblains in children; in short, she has cured more people in and about Lichfield within ten years than the doctors have kill'd in twenty; and that's a bold word.

AIMWELL. Has the lady been any other way useful in her generation?

BONNIFACE. Yes, sir, she has a daughter by Sir Charles, the finest woman in all our country, and the greatest fortune. She has a son too by her first husband Squire Sullen, who married a fine lady from London t'other day; if you please, sir, we'll drink his health?

AIMWELL. What sort of a man is he?

BONNIFACE. Why, sir, the man's well enough; says little, thinks less, and does – nothing at all, faith: But he's a man of a great estate, and values nobody.

AIMWELL. A sportsman, I suppose.

BONNIFACE. Yes, sir, he's a man of pleasure, he plays at whisk, and smokes his pipe eight and forty hours together sometimes.

AIMWELL. And married, you say?

BONNIFACE. Ay, and to a curious woman, sir, – But he's a – He wants it, here, sir. (*Pointing to his forehead.*)

AIMWELL. He has it there, you mean.

BONNIFACE. That's none of my business, he's my landlord, and so a man you know, would not, – But – Ecod, he's no better than – Sir, my humble service to you. (*Drinks.*) Tho' I value not a farthing what he can do to me; I pay him his rent at Quarter Day, I have a good running trade, I have but one daughter, and I can give her – but no matter for that.

AIMWELL. You're very happy, Mr. Bonniface, pray what other company have you in town?

BONNIFACE. A power of fine ladies, and then we have the French officers.

AIMWELL. O that's right, you have a good many of those gentlemen: Pray how do you like their company?

BONNIFACE. So well, as the saying is, that I could wish we had as many more of 'em, they're full of money, and pay double for everything they have; they know, sir, that we paid good round taxes for the taking of 'em, and so they are willing to reimburse us a little; one of 'em lodges in my house.

Enter ARCHER.

ARCHER. Landlord, there are some French gentlemen below that ask for you.

BONNIFACE. I'll wait on 'em; – Does your master stay long in town, as the saying is? (*To* ARCHER.)

ARCHER. I can't tell, as the saying is.

BONNIFACE. Come from London?

ARCHER. No.

BONNIFACE. Going to London, mayhap?

ARCHER. No.

BONNIFACE. An odd fellow this. I beg your worship's pardon, I'll wait on you in half a minute.

Exit.

AIMWELL. The coast's clear, I see, – Now my dear Archer, welcome to Lichfield.

ARCHER. I thank thee, my dear brother in iniquity.

AIMWELL. Iniquity! prithee leave canting, you need not change your style with your dress.

ARCHER. Don't mistake me, Aimwell, for 'tis still my maxim, that there is no scandal like rags, nor any crime so shameful as poverty.

AIMWELL. The world confesses it every day in its practice, tho' men won't own it for their opinion: who did that worthy Lord, my brother, single out of the side-box to sup with him t'other night?

ARCHER. Jack Handycraft, a handsome, well dress'd, mannerly, sharping rogue, who keeps the best company in town.

AIMWELL. Right, and pray who married my Lady Manslaughter t'other day, the great fortune?

ARCHER. Why, Nick Marrabone, a profess'd pick-pocket, and a good bowler; but he makes a handsome figure, and rides in his coach, that he formerly used to ride behind.

AIMWELL. But did you observe poor Jack Generous in the Park last week?

ARCHER. Yes, with his autumnal periwig, shading his melancholy face, his coat older than anything but its fashion, with one hand idle in his pocket, and with the other picking his useless teeth; and though the Mall was crowded with company, yet was poor Jack as single and solitary as a lion in a desert.

AIMWELL. And as much avoided, for no crime upon Earth but the want of money.

ARCHER. And that's enough; men must not be poor, idleness is the root of all evil; the world's wide enough, let 'em bustle; Fortune has taken the weak under her protection, but men of sense are left to their industry.

AIMWELL. Upon which topic we proceed, and I think luckily hitherto: Would not any man swear now that I am a man of quality, and you my servant, when if our intrinsic value were known –

ARCHER. Come, come, we are the men of intrinsic value, who can strike our fortunes out of ourselves, whose worth is independent of accidents in life, or revolutions in government; we have heads to get money, and hearts to spend it.

AIMWELL. As to our hearts, I grant'ye, they are as willing tits as any within twenty degrees; but I can have no great opinion of our heads from the service they have done us hitherto, unless it be that they have brought us from London hither to Lichfield, made me a Lord, and you my servant.

ARCHER. That's more than you could expect already. But what money have we left?

AIMWELL. But two hundred pound.

ARCHER. And our horses, clothes, rings, etc. – why we have very good fortunes now for moderate people; and let me tell you, besides, that this two hundred pound, with the experience that we are now masters of, is a better estate than the ten thousand we have spent. – Our friends indeed began to suspect that our pockets were low; but we came off with flying colours, showed no signs of want either in word or deed.

AIMWELL. Ay, and our going to Brussels was a good pretence
enough for our sudden disappearing; and I warrant you, our
friends imagine that we are gone a-volunteering.

ARCHER. Why faith, if this prospect fails, it must e'en come to
that, I am for venturing one of the hundreds if you will upon this
knight-errantry; but in case it should fail, we'll reserve th'other to
carry us to some counterscarp, where we may die as we liv'd in a
blaze.

AIMWELL. With all my heart; and we have liv'd justly, Archer, we
can't say that we have spent our fortunes, but that we have
enjoy'd 'em.

ARCHER. Right, so much pleasure for so much money, we have
had our pennyworths, and had I millions, I would go to the same
market again. O London, London! well, we have had our share,
and let us be thankful; Past pleasures, for ought I know are best,
such as we are sure of, those to come may disappoint us.

AIMWELL. It has often griev'd the heart of me, to see how some
inhumane wretches murther their kind fortunes; those that by
sacrificing all to one appetite, shall starve all the rest. – You shall
have some that live only in their palates, and in their sense of
tasting shall drown the other four: others are only epicures in
appearances, such who shall starve their nights to make a figure
a-days, and famish their own to feed the eyes of others: A contrary sort confine their pleasures to the dark, and contract their
spacious acres to the circuit of a muff-string.

ARCHER. Right; but they find the Indies in that spot where they
consume 'em, and I think your kind keepers have much the best
on't; for they indulge the most senses by one expense, there's
the seeing, hearing, and feeling amply gratified; and some philosophers will tell you, that from such a Commerce there arises a
sixth sense that gives infinitely more pleasure than the other five
put together.

AIMWELL. And to pass to the other extremity, of all keepers, I think
those the worst that keep their money.

ARCHER. Those are the most miserable wights in being, they destroy the rights of Nature, and disappoint the blessings of Providence: Give me a man that keeps his five senses keen and bright as his sword, that has 'em always drawn out in their just order and strength, with his reason as commander at the head of 'em, that detaches 'em by turns upon whatever party of pleasure agreeably offers, and commands 'em to retreat upon the least appearance of disadvantage or danger: – For my part I can stick to my bottle, while my wine, my company, and my reason holds good; I can be charm'd with Sappho's singing without falling in love with her face; I love hunting, but would not, like Acteon, be eaten up by my own dogs; I love a fine house, but let another keep it; and just so I love a fine woman.

AIMWELL. In that last particular you have the better of me.

ARCHER. Ay, you're such an amorous puppy, that I'm afraid you'll spoil our sport; you can't counterfeit the passion without feeling it.

AIMWELL. Tho' the whining part be out of doors in town, 'tis still in force with the country ladies; – And let me tell you Frank, the fool in that passion shall outdo the knave at any time.

ARCHER. Well, I won't dispute it now, you command for the day, and so I submit; – At Nottingham you know I am to be master.

AIMWELL. And at Lincoln I again.

ARCHER. Then at Norwich I mount, which, I think, shall be our last stage; for if we fail there, we'll embark for Holland, bid adieu to Venus, and welcome Mars.

AIMWELL. A match!

Enter BONNIFACE

Mum.

BONNIFACE. What will your worship please to have for supper?

AIMWELL. What have you got?

BONNIFACE. Sir, we have a delicate piece of beef in the pot, and a pig at the fire.

AIMWELL. Good supper-meat, I must confess, – I can't eat beef, landlord.

ARCHER. And I hate pig.

AIMWELL. Hold your prating, sirrah, do you know who you are?

BONNIFACE. Please to bespeak something else, I have every thing in the house.

AIMWELL. Have you any veal?

BONNIFACE. Veal! Sir, we had a delicate loin of veal on Wednesday last.

AIMWELL. Have you got any fish or wildfowl?

BONNIFACE. As for fish, truly sir, we are an inland town, and indifferently provided with fish, that's the truth on't, and then for wildfowl, – we have a delicate couple of rabbits.

AIMWELL. Get me the rabbits fricasy'd.

BONNIFACE. Fricasy'd! Lard, sir, they'll eat much better smother'd with onions.

ARCHER. Pshaw! damn your onions.

AIMWELL. Again, sirrah! – well, landlord, what you please; but hold, I have a small charge of money, and your house is so full of strangers, that I believe it may be safer in your custody than mine; for when this fellow of mine gets drunk, he minds nothing. – Here, sirrah, reach me the strong box.

ARCHER. Yes, sir, – This will give us a reputation. (*Aside*.)

Brings the box.

AIMWELL. Here, landlord, the locks are sealed down both for your security and mine; it holds somewhat above two hundred pound; if you doubt it, I'll count it to you after supper; but be sure you lay it where I may have it at a minute's warning; for my affairs are a little dubious at present, perhaps I may be gone in half an hour, perhaps I may be your guest till the best part of that be spent; and pray order your ostler to keep my horses always saddled; but one thing above the rest I must beg, that you would let this fellow have none of your *Anno Domini*, as you call it; – For he's the most insufferable sot – here, sirrah, light me to my chamber.

Exit lighted by ARCHER.

BONNIFACE. Cherry, daughter Cherry!

Enter CHERRY.

CHERRY. D'ye call, Father?

BONNIFACE. Ay, child, you must lay by this box for the gentle-man, 'tis full of money.

CHERRY. Money! all that money! why, sure father the gentleman comes to be chosen parliament-man. Who is he?

BONNIFACE. I don't know what to make of him, he talks of keeping his horses ready saddled, and of going perhaps at a minute's warning, or of staying perhaps till the best part of this be spent.

CHERRY. Ay, ten to one, father, he's a highwayman.

BONNIFACE. A highwayman! upon my life, girl, you have hit it, and this box is some new purchased booty. – Now could we find him out, the money were ours.

CHERRY. He don't belong to our gang?

BONNIFACE. What horses have they?

CHERRY. The master rides upon a black.

BONNIFACE. A black! ten to one the màn upon the black mare; and since he don't belong to our Fraternity, we may betray him with a safe conscience; I don't think it lawful to harbour any rogues but my own. – Look'ye, child, as the saying is, we must go cunningly to work, proofs we must have, the gentleman's servant loves drink, I'll ply him that way, and ten to one loves a wench; you must work him t'other way.

CHERRY. Father, would you have me give my secret for his?

BONNIFACE. Consider, child, there's two hundred pound to boot.

Ringing without.

Coming, coming. – Child, mind your business.

CHERRY. What a rogue is my father! my father! I deny it. – My mother was a good, generous, free-hearted woman, and I can't tell how far her good nature might have extended for the good of her children. This landlord of mine, for I think I can call him no more, would betray his guest, and debauch his daughter into the bargain, – by a footman too!

Enter ARCHER.

ARCHER. What footman, pray, mistress, is so happy as to be the subject of your contemplation?

CHERRY. Whoever he is, friend, he'll be but little the better for't.

ARCHER. I hope so, for I'm sure you did not think of me.

CHERRY. Suppose I had?

ARCHER. Why then you're but even with me; for the minute I came in, I was a considering in what manner I should make love to you.

CHERRY. Love to me, friend!

ARCHER. Yes, child.

CHERRY. Child! Manners; if you kept a little more distance, friend, it would become you much better.

ARCHER. Distance! good night, sauce-box. (*Going.*)

CHERRY. A pretty fellow! I like his pride, – Sir, pray, sir, you see, sir, (ARCHER *returns.*) I have the credit to be entrusted with your master's fortune here, which sets me a degree above his footman; I hope, sir, you an't affronted.

ARCHER. Let me look you full in the face, and I'll tell you whether you can affront me or no. – S'death, child, you have a pair of delicate eyes, and you don't know what to do with 'em.

CHERRY. Why, sir, don't I see every body?

ARCHER. Ay, but if some women had 'em, they would kill everybody. – Prithee, instruct me, I would fain make love to you, but I don't know what to say.

CHERRY. Why, did you never make love to any body before?

ARCHER. Never to a person of your figure, I can assure you, madam, my addresses have been always confin'd to people within my own sphere, I never aspir'd so high before.

(A Song.)

But you look so bright,
And are dress'd so tight,
That a man would swear you're right,
*   As arm was e'er laid over.*

Such an air
You freely wear
To ensnare,
*   As makes each guest a lover!*

Since then, my dear, I'm your guest,
Prithee give me of the best
Of what is ready drest:
*   Since then, my dear, etc.*

CHERRY. What can I think of this man? (*Aside.*) Will you give me that song, sir?

ARCHER. Ay, my dear, take it while 'tis warm. (*Kisses her.*) Death and fire! her lips are honeycombs.

CHERRY. And I wish there had been bees too, to have stung you for your impudence.

ARCHER. There's a swarm of Cupids, my little Venus, that has done the business much better.

CHERRY. This fellow is misbegotten as well as I. (*Aside.*) What's your name, sir?

ARCHER. Name! I gad, I have forgot it. (*Aside.*) Oh! Martin.

CHERRY. Where were you born?

ARCHER. In St. Martin's Parish.

CHERRY. What was your father?

ARCHER. St. Martin's Parish.

CHERRY. Then, friend, good night.

ARCHER. I hope not.

CHERRY. You may depend upon't.

ARCHER. Upon what?

CHERRY. That you're very impudent.

ARCHER. That you're very handsome.

CHERRY. That you're a footman.

ARCHER. That you're an angel.

CHERRY. I shall be rude.

ARCHER. So shall I.

CHERRY. Let go my hand.

ARCHER. Give me a kiss.

> *Kisses her.*

> *Call without,* 'Cherry, Cherry.'

CHERRY. I'm – My Father calls; you plaguy devil, how durst you stop my breath so? – Offer to follow me one step, if you dare.

ARCHER. A fair challenge by this light; this is a pretty fair opening of an adventure; but we are knight-errants, and so Fortune be our guide.

> *Exit.*

> *The End of the First Act.*

Act II

[Scene i]

Scene, a gallery in Lady Bountiful's house. MRS. SULLEN *and* DORINDA *meeting.*

DORINDA. Morrow, my dear sister; are you for church this morning?

MRS SULLEN. Any where to pray; for Heaven alone can help me: But, I think, Dorinda, there's no form of prayer in the Liturgy against bad husbands.

DORINDA. But there's a form of law in Doctors-Commons; and I swear, sister Sullen, rather than see you thus continually discontented, I would advise you to apply to that: For besides the part that I bear in your vexatious broils, as being sister to the husband, and friend to the wife; your example gives me such an impression of matrimony, that I shall be apt to condemn my person to a long vacation all its life. – But supposing, madam, that you brought it to a case of separation, what can you urge against your husband? My brother is, first, the most constant man alive.

MRS SULLEN. The most constant husband, I grant'ye.

DORINDA. He never sleeps from you.

MRS SULLEN. No, he always sleeps with me.

DORINDA. He allows you a maintenance suitable to your quality.

MRS SULLEN. A maintenance! do you take me, madam, for an hospital child, that I must sit down, and bless my benefactors for meat, drink and clothes? As I take it, madam, I brought your brother ten thousand pounds, out of which, I might expect some pretty things, called pleasures.

DORINDA. You share in all the pleasures that the country affords.

MRS SULLEN. Country pleasures! Racks and torments! dost think, child, that my limbs were made for leaping of ditches, and clamb'ring over stiles; or that my parents wisely foreseeing my future happiness in country pleasures, had early instructed me in the rural accomplishments of drinking fat ale, playing at whisk, and smoking tobacco with my husband; or of spreading of plasters, brewing of diet-drinks, and stilling rosemary-water with the good old gentlewoman, my mother-in-law.

DORINDA. I'm sorry, madam, that it is not more in our power to divert you; I could wish indeed that our entertainments were a little more polite, or your taste a little less refin'd: But, pray, madam, how came the poets and philosophers that labour'd so much in hunting after pleasure, to place it at last in a country life?

MRS SULLEN. Because they wanted money, child, to find out the pleasures of the town: Did you ever see a poet or philosopher worth ten thousand pound; if you can show me such a man, I'll lay you fifty pound you'll find him somewhere within the weekly bills. – Not that I disapprove rural pleasures, as the poets have painted them; in their landscape every Phillis has her Coridon, every murmuring stream, and every flowery mead gives fresh alarms to love. – Besides, you'll find, that their couples were never married: – But yonder I see my Coridon, and a sweet swain it is, Heaven knows. – Come, Dorinda, don't be angry, he's my husband, and your brother; and between both is he not a sad brute?

DORINDA. I have nothing to say to your part of him, you're the best judge.

MRS SULLEN. O sister, sister! if ever you marry, beware of a sullen, silent sot, one that's always musing, but never thinks: There's some diversion in a talking blockhead; and since a woman must wear chains, I would have the pleasure of hearing 'em rattle a little. – Now you shall see, but take this by the way; – He came home this morning at his usual hour of four, waken'd me out of a sweet dream of something else, by tumbling over the tea-table, which he broke all to pieces, after his man and he had rowl'd about the room like sick passengers in a storm, he comes flounce into bed, dead as a salmon into a fishmonger's basket; his feet cold as ice, his breath hot as a furnace, and his hands and his face as greasy as his flannel nightcap. – Oh matrimony! – He tosses up the clothes with a barbarous swing over his shoulders, disorders the whole economy of my bed, leaves me half naked, and my whole night's comfort is the tuneable serenade of that wakeful nightingale, his nose. – O the pleasure of counting the melancholy clock by a snoring husband! But now, sister, you shall see how handsomely, being a well-bred man, he will beg my pardon.

Enter SULLEN.

SULLEN. My head aches consumedly.

MRS SULLEN. Will you be pleased, my dear, to drink tea with us this morning? it may do your head good.

SULLEN. No.

DORINDA. Coffee? Brother.

SULLEN. Pshaw.

MRS SULLEN. Will you please to dress and go to church with me, the air may help you.

SULLEN. Scrub.

Enter SCRUB.

SCRUB. Sir.

SULLEN. What day o'th week is this?

SCRUB. Sunday, an't please your Worship.

SULLEN. Sunday! bring me a dram, and d'ye hear, set out the venison-pasty, and a tankard of strong beer upon the hall-table, I'll go to breakfast.

Going.

DORINDA. Stay, stay, brother, you shan't get off so; you were very naughty last night, and must make your wife reparation; come, come, brother, won't you ask pardon?

SULLEN. For what?

DORINDA. For being drunk last night.

SULLEN. I can afford it, can't I?

MRS SULLEN. But I can't, sir.

SULLEN. Then you may let it alone.

MRS SULLEN. But I must tell you, sir, that this is not to be born.

SULLEN. I'm glad on't.

MRS SULLEN. What is the reason, sir, that you use me thus
inhumanely?

SULLEN. Scrub?

SCRUB. Sir.

SULLEN. Get things ready to shave my head.

Exit.

MRS SULLEN. Have a care of coming near his temples, Scrub,
for fear you meet something there that may turn the edge of
your razor. – Inveterate stupidity! did you ever know so hard, so
obstinate a spleen as his? O sister, sister! I shall never ha' good of
the beast till I get him to town; London, dear London is the place
for managing and breaking a husband.

DORINDA. And has not a husband the same opportunities there for
humbling a wife?

MRS SULLEN. No, no, child, 'tis a standing maxim in conjugal
discipline, that when a man would enslave his wife, he hurries her
into the country; and when a lady would be arbitrary with her
husband, she wheedles her booby up to town. – A man dare not
play the tyrant in London, because there are so many examples to
encourage the subject to rebel. O Dorinda, Dorinda! a fine
woman may do anything in London: O'my conscience, she may
raise an army of forty thousand men.

DORINDA. I fancy, sister, you have a mind to be trying your power
that way here in Lichfield; you have drawn the French count to
your colours already.

MRS SULLEN. The French are a people that can't live without their gallantries.

DORINDA. And some English that I know, sister, are not averse to such amusements.

MRS SULLEN. Well, sister, since the truth must out, it may do as well now as hereafter; I think one way to rouse my lethargic sottish husband, is, to give him a rival; security begets negligence in all people, and men must be alarm'd to make 'em alert in their duty: women are like pictures of no value in the hands of a fool, till he hears men of sense bid high for the purchase.

DORINDA. This might do, sister, if my brother's understanding were to be convinc'd into a passion for you; but I fancy there's a natural aversion of his side; and I fancy, sister, that you don't come much behind him, if you dealt fairly.

MRS SULLEN. I own it, we are united contradictions, fire and water: But I could be contented, with a great many other wives, to humour the censorious mob, and give the world an appearance of living well with my husband, could I bring him but to dissemble a little kindness to keep me in countenance.

DORINDA. But how do you know, sister, but that instead of rousing your husband by this artifice to a counterfeit kindness, he should awake in a real fury?

MRS SULLEN. Let him: – If I can't entice him to the one, I would provoke him to the other.

DORINDA. But how must I behave myself between ye?

MRS SULLEN. You must assist me.

DORINDA. What, against my own brother!

MRS SULLEN. He's but half a brother, and I'm your entire friend: If I go a step beyond the bounds of honour, leave me; till then I expect you should go along with me in everything, while I trust my honour in your hands, you may trust your brother's in mine. – The Count is to dine here today.

DORINDA. 'Tis a strange thing, sister, that I can't like that man.

MRS SULLEN. You like nothing, your time is not come; Love and
death have their fatalities, and strike home one time or other:
You'll pay for all one day, I warrant'ye. But, come, my Lady's tea
is ready, and 'tis almost church-time.

Exeunt.

[Act II, Scene ii]

Scene, the inn. Enter AIMWELL *dress'd, and* ARCHER.

AIMWELL. And was she the daughter of the house?

ARCHER. The landlord is so blind as to think so; but I dare swear
she has better blood in her veins.

AIMWELL. Why dost think so?

ARCHER. Because the baggage has a pert *Je ne sais quoi,* she reads
plays, keeps a monkey, and is troubled with vapours.

AIMWELL. By which discoveries I guess that you know more of her.

ARCHER. Not yet, faith, the lady gives herself airs, forsooth,
nothing under a gentleman.

AIMWELL. Let me take her in hand.

ARCHER. Say one word more o'that, and I'll declare myself, spoil
your sport there, and every where else; look'ye, Aimwell, every
man in his own sphere.

AIMWELL. Right; and therefore you must pimp for your master.

ARCHER. In the usual forms, good sir, after I have serv'd my self.
But to our business: – You are so well dress'd, Tom, and make
so handsome a figure, that I fancy you may do execution in a
country church; the exterior part strikes first, and you're in the
right to make that impression favourable.

AIMWELL. There's something in that which may turn to
advantage: The appearance of a stranger in a country church
draws as many gazers as a blazing star; no sooner he comes into
the cathedral, but a train of whispers runs buzzing round the
congregation in a moment; – Who is he? whence comes he?
do you know him? – Then I, sir, tips me the verger with half a
crown; he pockets the simony, and inducts me into the best pew
in the church, I pull out my snuff-box, turn myself round, bow to
the Bishop, or the Dean, if he be the commanding officer; single
out a beauty, rivet both my eyes to hers, set my nose a bleeding
by the strength of imagination, and show the whole church my
concern by my endeavouring to hide it; after the sermon, the
whole town gives me to her for a lover, and by persuading the
lady that I am a-dying for her, the tables are turn'd, and she in
good earnest falls in love with me.

ARCHER. There's nothing in this, Tom, without a precedent; but
instead of riveting your eyes to a beauty, try to fix 'em upon a
fortune, that's our business at present.

AIMWELL. Pshaw, no woman can be a beauty without a fortune. –
Let me alone, for I am a marksman.

ARCHER. Tom.

AIMWELL. Ay.

ARCHER. When were you at church before, pray?

AIMWELL. Um – I was there at the Coronation.

ARCHER. And how can you expect a blessing by going to church
now?

AIMWELL. Blessing! nay, Frank, I ask but for a wife.

Exit.

ARCHER. Truly the man is not very unreasonable in his demands.

Exit at the opposite door. Enter BONNIFACE *and* CHERRY.

BONNIFACE. Well daughter, as the saying is, have you brought
Martin to confess?

CHERRY. Pray, father, don't put me upon getting any thing out of a man; I'm but young you know, father, and I don't understand wheedling.

BONNIFACE. Young! why you jade, as the saying is, can any woman wheedle that is not young? your mother was useless at five and twenty; not wheedle! would you make your mother a whore and me a cuckold, as the saying is? I tell you his silence confesses it, and his master spends his money so freely, and is so much a gentleman every manner of way that he must be a highwayman.

Enter GIBBET in a cloak.

GIBBET. Landlord, landlord, is the coast clear?

BONNIFACE. O, Mr. Gibbet, what's the news?

GIBBET. No matter, ask no questions, all fair and honourable, here, my dear Cherry – (*Gives her a bag.*) Two hundred sterling pounds, as good as any that ever hang'd or sav'd a rogue; lay 'em by with the rest, and here – Three wedding or mourning rings, 'tis much the same you know – Here, two silver-hilted swords; I took those from fellows that never show any part of their swords but the hilts: Here is a diamond necklace which the lady hid in the privatest place in the coach, but I found it out: This gold watch I took from a pawnbroker's wife; it was left in her hands by a person of quality, there's the arms upon the case.

CHERRY. But who had you the money from?

GIBBET. Ah! poor woman! I pitied her; – From a poor lady just elop'd from her husband, she had made up her cargo, and was bound for Ireland, as hard as she could drive; she told me of her husband's barbarous usage, and so I left her half a crown: But I had almost forgot, my dear Cherry, I have a present for you.

CHERRY. What is't?

GIBBET. A pot of cereuse, my child, that I took out of a lady's under pocket.

CHERRY. What, Mr. Gibbet, do you think that I paint?

GIBBET. Why, you jade, your betters do; I'm sure the lady that I took it from had a coronet upon her handkerchief. – Here, take my cloak, and go, secure the premisses.

CHERRY. I will secure 'em.

Exit.

BONNIFACE. But, heark'ye, where's Hounslow and Bagshot?

GIBBET. They'll be here tonight.

BONNIFACE. D'ye know of any other gentlemen o'the pad on this road?

GIBBET. No.

BONNIFACE. I fancy that I have two that lodge in the house just now.

GIBBET. The devil! how d'ye smoke 'em?

BONNIFACE. Why, the one is gone to church.

GIBBET. That's suspicious, I must confess.

BONNIFACE. And the other is now in his master's chamber; he pretends to be servant to the other, we'll call him out, and pump him a little.

GIBBET. With all my heart.

BONNIFACE. Mr. Martin, Mr. Martin?

Enter MARTIN *combing a periwig, and singing.*

GIBBET. The roads are consumed deep; I'm as dirty as old Brentford at Christmas. – A good pretty fellow that; who's servant are you, friend?

ARCHER. My master's.

GIBBET. Really?

ARCHER. Really.

GIBBET. That's much. The fellow has been at the bar by his evasions: but, pray, sir, what is your master's name?

ARCHER. *Tall, all dall;* (*Sings and combs the periwig.*) This is the most obstinate churl –

GIBBET. I ask you his name?

ARCHER. Name, sir, – *Tall, all dal* – I never ask'd him his name in my life. *Tall, all dall.*

BONNIFACE. What think you now?

GIBBET. Plain, plain, he talks now as if he were before a judge: But, pray, friend, which way does your master travel?

ARCHER. A horseback.

GIBBET. Very well again, an old offender, right; – But, I mean does he go upwards or downwards?

ARCHER. Downwards, I fear, sir: *Tall, all.*

GIBBET. I'm afraid my fate will be a contrary way.

BONNIFACE. Ha, ha, ha! Mr. Martin you're very arch. – This gentleman is only travelling towards Chester, and would be glad of your company, that's all. – Come, Captain, you'll stay tonight, I suppose; I'll show you a chamber – Come, Captain.

GIBBET. Farewell, friend –

Exit.

ARCHER. Captain, your servant. – Captain! a pretty fellow; s'death, I wonder that the officers of the army don't conspire to beat all scoundrels in red, but their own.

Enter CHERRY.

CHERRY. Gone! and Martin here! I hope he did not listen; I would have the merit of the discovery all my own, because I would oblige him to love me. (*Aside.*) Mr. Martin, who was that man with my father?

ARCHER. Some recruiting sergeant, or whipped-out trooper, I suppose.

CHERRY. All's safe, I find. (*Aside.*)

ARCHER. Come, my dear, have you con'd over the Catechise
    I taught you last night?

CHERRY. Come, question me.

ARCHER. What is love?

CHERRY. Love is I know not what, it comes I know not how, and
    goes I know not when.

ARCHER. Very well, an apt scholar. (*Chucks her under the chin.*) Where
    does love enter?

CHERRY. Into the eyes.

ARCHER. And where go out?

CHERRY. I won't tell'ye.

ARCHER. What are objects of that passion?

CHERRY. Youth, beauty, and clean linen.

ARCHER. The reason?

CHERRY. The two first are fashionable in Nature, and the third at
    Court.

ARCHER. That's my dear: What are the signs and tokens of that
    passion?

CHERRY. A stealing look, a stammering tongue, words improbable,
    designs impossible, and actions impracticable.

ARCHER. That's my good child, kiss me. – What must a lover do to
    obtain his mistress?

CHERRY. He must adore the person that disdains him, he must
    bribe the chambermaid that betrays him, and court the footman
    that laughs at him; – He must, he must –

ARCHER. Nay, child, I must whip you if you don't mind your
    lesson; he must treat his –

CHERRY. O, ay, he must treat his enemies with respect, his
    friends with indifference, and all the world with contempt;

he must suffer much, and fear more; he must desire much, and hope little; in short, he must embrace his ruin, and throw himself away.

ARCHER. Had ever man so hopeful a pupil as mine? come, my dear, why is love call'd a riddle?

CHERRY. Because being blind, he leads those that see, and though a child, he governs a man.

ARCHER. Mighty well. – And why is love pictur'd blind?

CHERRY. Because the painters out of the weakness or privilege of their art chose to hide those eyes that they could not draw.

ARCHER. That's my dear little scholar, kiss me again. And why should love, that's a child, govern a man?

CHERRY. Because that a child is the end of love.

ARCHER. And so ends Love's Catechism. – And now, my dear, we'll go in, and make my master's bed.

CHERRY. Hold, hold, Mr. Martin, – You have taken a great deal of pains to instruct me, and what d'ye think I have learnt by it?

ARCHER. What?

CHERRY. That your discourse and your habit are contradictions, and it would be nonsense in me to believe you a footman any longer.

ARCHER. 'Oons, what a witch it is!

CHERRY. Depend upon this, sir, nothing in this garb shall ever tempt me; for though I was born to servitude, I hate it: Own your condition, swear you love me, and then –

ARCHER. And then we shall go make the bed.

CHERRY. Yes.

ARCHER. You must know then, that I am born a gentleman, my education was liberal; but I went to London a younger brother, fell into the hands of sharpers, who stripped me of my money, my friends disown'd me, and now my necessity brings me to what you see.

CHERRY. Then take my hand – promise to marry me before you sleep, and I'll make you master of two thousand pound.

ARCHER. How!

CHERRY. Two thousand pound that I have this minute in my own custody; so throw off your livery this instant, and I'll go find a parson.

ARCHER. What said you? A parson!

CHERRY. What! do you scruple?

ARCHER. Scruple! no, no, but – two thousand pound you say?

CHERRY. And better.

ARCHER. S'death, what shall I do – but heark'ee, child, what need you make me master of your self and money, when you may have the same pleasure out of me, and still keep your fortune in your hands.

CHERRY. Then you won't marry me?

ARCHER. I would marry you, but –

CHERRY. O sweet, sir, I'm your humble servant, you're fairly caught, would you persuade me that any gentleman who could bear the scandal of wearing a livery, would refuse two thousand pound let the condition be what it would – no, no, sir, – but I hope you'll pardon the freedom I have taken, since it was only to inform myself of the respect that I ought to pay you. (*Going.*)

ARCHER. Fairly bit, by Jupiter – hold, hold, and have you actually two thousand pound?

CHERRY. Sir, I have my secrets as well as you – when you please to be more open, I shall be more free, and be assur'd that I have discoveries that will match yours, be what they will – in the mean while be satisfied that no discovery I make shall ever hurt you, but beware of my father. –

Exit.

ARCHER. So – we're like to have as many adventures in our inn, as Don Quixote had in his – let me see, – two thousand pound!

if the wench would promise to die when the money were spent, I gad, one would marry her, but the fortune may go off in a year or two, and the wife may live – Lord knows how long? then an innkeeper's daughter;.ay that's the devil – there my pride brings me off.

For whatsoe'er the sages charge on pride
The angels fall, and twenty faults beside,
On Earth I'm sure, 'mong us of mortal calling,
Pride saves man oft, and woman too from falling.

Exit.

End of the Second Act.

Act III

[Scene i]

Scene continues. Enter MRS SULLEN, DORINDA.

MRS SULLEN. Ha, ha, ha, my dear sister, let me embrace thee, – now we are friends indeed! for I shall have a secret of yours, as a pledge for mine – now you'll be good for something, I shall have you conversable in the subjects of the sex.

DORINDA. But do you think that I am so weak as to fall in love with a fellow at first sight?

MRS SULLEN. Pshaw! now you spoil all, why should not we be as free in our friendships as the men? I warrant you the gentleman has got to his confidant already, has avow'd his passion, toasted your health, call'd you ten thousand angels, has run over your lips, eyes, neck, shape, air and every thing, in a description that warms their mirth to a second enjoyment.

DORINDA. Your hand, sister, I an't well.

MRS SULLEN. So, – she's breeding already – come child up with it – hem a little – so – now tell me, don't you like the gentleman that we saw at church just now?

DORINDA. The man's well enough.

MRS SULLEN. Well enough! is he not a demigod, a Narcissus, a star, the man i'the moon?

DORINDA. O sister, I'm extremely ill.

MRS SULLEN. Shall I send to your mother, child, for a little of her cephalic plaister to put to the soles of your feet, or shall I send to the gentleman for something for you? – Come, unlace your stays, unbosom your self – the man is perfectly a pretty fellow, I saw him when he first came into church.

DORINDA. I saw him too, sister, and with an air that shone, methought like rays about his person.

MRS SULLEN. Well said, up with it.

DORINDA. No forward coquett behaviour, no airs to set him off, no studied looks nor artful posture, ⊤ but Nature did it all –

MRS SULLEN. Better and better – one touch more – come. –

DORINDA. But then his looks – did you observe his eyes?

MRS SULLEN. Yes, yes, I did his eyes, – well, what of his eyes?

DORINDA. Sprightly, but not wand'ring; they seem'd to view, but never gaz'd on any thing but me – and then his looks so humble were, and yet so noble, that they aim'd to tell me that he could with pride die at my feet, tho' he scorn'd slavery anywhere else.

MRS SULLEN. The physic works purely – How d'ye find your self now, my dear?

DORINDA. Hem! much better, my dear – O here comes our mercury!

Enter SCRUB.

Well Scrub, what news of the gentleman?

SCRUB. Madam, I have brought you a packet of news.

DORINDA. Open it quickly, come.

SCRUB. In the first place I enquir'd who the gentleman was? They told me he was a stranger, Secondly, I ask'd what the gentleman was, they answer'd and said, that they never saw him before. Thirdly, I enquir'd what countryman he was, they replied 'twas more than they knew. Fourthly, I demanded whence he came, their answer was, they could not tell. And fifthly, I ask'd whither he went, and they replied they knew nothing of the matter, – and this is all I could learn.

MRS SULLEN. But what do the people say, can't they guess?

SCRUB. Why some think he's a spy, some guess he's a mountebank, some say one thing, some another; but for my own part, I believe he's a Jesuit.

DORINDA. A Jesuit! why a Jesuit?

SCRUB. Because he keeps his horses always ready saddled, and his footman talks French.

MRS SULLEN. His footman!

SCRUB. Ay, he and the Count's footman were jabbering French like two intreaguing ducks in a mill-pond, and I believe they talk'd of me, for they laugh'd consumedly.

DORINDA. What sort of livery has the footman?

SCRUB. Livery! Lord, madam, I took him for a captain, he's so bedizen'd with lace, and then he has tops to his shoes, up to his mid leg, a silver-headed cane dangling at his knuckles, – he carries his hands in his pockets just so – (*Walks in the French air.*) and has a fine long periwig tied up in a bag – Lord, madam, he's clear another sort of man than I.

MRS SULLEN. That may easily be – but what shall we do now, sister?

DORINDA. I have it – This fellow has a world of simplicity, and some cunning, the first hides the latter by abundance – Scrub.

SCRUB. Madam.

DORINDA. We have a great mind to know who this gentleman is, only for our satisfaction.

SCRUB. Yes, madam, it would be a satisfaction, no doubt.

DORINDA. You must go and get acquainted with his footman, and invite him hither to drink a bottle of your ale, because you're butler today.

SCRUB. Yes, madam, I am butler every Sunday.

MRS SULLEN. O brave, sister, O my conscience, you understand the mathematics already – 'tis the best plot in the world, your mother, you know, will be gone to church, my spouse will be got

to the ale-house with his scoundrels, and the house will be
our own – so we drop in by accident and ask the fellow some
questions ourselves. In the country you know any stranger is
company, and we're glad to take up with the butler in a country
dance, and happy if he'll do us the favour.

SCRUB. Oh! Madam, you wrong me, I never refus'd your ladyship
the favour in my life.

Enter GIPSEY.

GIPSEY. Ladies, dinner's upon table.

DORINDA. Scrub, We'll excuse your waiting – Go where we
order'd you.

SCRUB. I shall.

Exeunt.

[Act III, Scene ii]

Scene changes to the inn. Enter AIMWELL *and* ARCHER.

ARCHER. Well, Tom, I find you're a marksman.

AIMWELL. A marksman! who so blind could be, as not discern a
swan among the ravens?

ARCHER. Well, but heark'ee, Aimwell.

AIMWELL. Aimwell! call me Oroondates, Cesario, Amadis, all that
romance can in a lover paint, and then I'll answer. O Archer,
I read her thousands in her looks, she look'd like Ceres in her
harvest, corn, wine and oil, milk and honey, gardens, groves
and purling streams play'd on her plenteous face.

ARCHER. Her face! her pocket, you mean; the corn, wine and oil
lies there. In short, she has ten thousand pound, that's the English
on't.

AIMWELL. Her eyes –

ARCHER. Are demi-cannons to be sure, so I won't stand their battery.

Going.

AIMWELL. Pray excuse me, my passion must have vent.   .

ARCHER. Passion! what a plague, d'ee think these romantic airs will do our business? Were my temper as extravagant as yours, my adventures have something more romantic by half.

AIMWELL. Your adventures!

ARCHER. Yes,

The nymph that with her twice ten hundred pounds
With brazen engine hot, and quoif clear starch'd
Can fire the guest in warming of the bed –

There's a touch of sublime Milton for you, and the subject but an innkeeper's daughter; I can play with a girl as an angler do's with his fish; he keeps it at the end of his line, runs it up the stream, and down the stream, till at last, he brings it to hand, tickles the trout, and so whips it into his basket.

Enter BONNIFACE.

BONNIFACE. Mr. Martin, as the saying is – yonder's an honest fellow below, my Lady Bountiful's butler, who begs the honour that you would go home with him and see his cellar.

ARCHER. Do my baisemains to the gentleman, and tell him I will do my self the honour to wait on him immediately.

Exit BONNIFACE.

AIMWELL. What do I hear? soft Orpheus play, and fair Toftida sing?

ARCHER. Pshaw! damn your raptures, I tell you here's a pump going to be put into the vessel, and the ship will get into harbour, my life on't. You say there's another lady very handsome there.

AIMWELL. Yes, faith.

ARCHER. I'm in love with her already.

AIMWELL. Can't you give me a bill upon Cherry in the meantime?

ARCHER. No, no, friend, all her corn, wine and oil is ingross'd to my market. – And once more I warn you to keep your anchorage clear of mine, for if you fall foul of me, by this light you shall go to the bottom. – What! make prize of my little frigate, while I am upon the guise for you.

Exit. Enter BONNIFACE.

AIMWELL. Well, well, I won't – landlord, have you any tolerable company in the house, I don't care for dining alone.

BONNIFACE. Yes, sir, there's a captain below; as the saying is, that arrived about an hour ago.

AIMWELL. Gentlemen of his coat are welcome everywhere; will you make him a compliment from me, and tell him I should be glad of his company.

BONNIFACE. Who shall I tell him, sir, would. –

AIMWELL. Ha! that stroke was well thrown in – I'm only a traveller like himself, and would be glad of his company, that's all.

BONNIFACE. I obey your commands, as the saying is.

Exit. Enter ARCHER.

ARCHER. S'death! I had forgot, what title will you give yourself?

AIMWELL. My brother's to be sure, he would never give me any thing else, so I'll make bold with his honour this bout – you know the rest of your cue.

Exit BONNIFACE.

ARCHER. Ay, ay.

Enter GIBBET.

GIBBET. Sir, I'm yours.

AIMWELL. 'Tis more than I deserve, sir, for I don't know you.

GIBBET. I don't wonder at that, sir, for you never saw me before, I hope. (*Aside.*)

AIMWELL. And pray, sir, how came I by the honour of seeing you now?

GIBBET. Sir, I scorn to intrude upon any gentleman – but my landlord –

AIMWELL. O, sir, I ask your pardon, you're the captain he told me of.

GIBBET. At your service, sir.

AIMWELL. What regiment, may I be so bold?

GIBBET. A marching regiment, sir, an old corps.

AIMWELL. Very old, if your coat be regimental. (*Aside.*) You have serv'd abroad, sir?

GIBBET. Yes, sir, in the plantations, 'twas my lot to be sent into the worst service, I would have quitted it indeed, but a man of honour, you know – Besides 'twas for the good of my country that I should be abroad – any thing for the good of one's country – I'm a Roman for that.

AIMWELL. One of the first, I'll lay my life. (*Aside.*) You found the West Indies very hot, sir?

GIBBET. Ay, sir, too hot for me.

AIMWELL. Pray, sir, haven't I seen your face at Will's coffee-house?

GIBBET. Yes, sir, and at White's too.

AIMWELL. And where is your company now, captain?

GIBBET. They an't come yet.

AIMWELL. Why, d'ye expect 'em here?

GIBBET. They'll be here tonight, sir.

AIMWELL. Which way do they march?

GIBBET. Across the country – the Devil's in't, if I han't said enough to encourage him to declare – but I'm afraid he's not right, I must tack about.

AIMWELL. Is your company to quarter in Lichfield?

GIBBET. In this house, sir.

AIMWELL. What! all?

GIBBET. My company's but thin, ha, ha, ha, we are but three, ha, ha, ha.

AIMWELL. You're merry, sir.

GIBBET. Ay, sir, you must excuse me, sir, I understand the world, especially, the art of travelling; I don't care, sir, for answering questions directly upon the road – for I generally ride with a charge about me.

AIMWELL. Three or four, I believe. (*Aside.*)

GIBBET. I am credibly inform'd that there are highwaymen upon this quarter, not, sir, that I could suspect a gentleman of your figure – But truly, sir, I have got such a way of evasion upon the road, that I don't care for speaking truth to any man.

AIMWELL. Your caution may be necessary – Then I presume you're no captain?

GIBBET. Not I, sir, captain is a good travelling name, and so I take it; it stops a great many foolish inquiries that are generally made about gentlemen that travel, it gives a man an air of something, and makes the drawers obedient – And thus far I am a captain, and no farther.

AIMWELL. And pray, sir, what is your true profession?

GIBBET. O, sir, you must excuse me – upon my word, sir, I don't think it safe to tell you.

AIMWELL. Ha, ha, ha, upon my word I commend you.

Enter BONNIFACE.

Well, Mr. Bonniface, what's the news?

BONNIFACE. There's another gentleman below, as the saying is, that hearing you were but two, would be glad to make the third man if you would give him leave.

AIMWELL. What is he?

BONNIFACE. A clergyman, as the saying is.

AIMWELL. A clergyman! is he really a clergyman? or is it only his travelling name, as my friend the captain has it.

BONNIFACE. O, sir, he's a priest and chaplain to the French officers in town.

AIMWELL. Is he a Frenchman?

BONNIFACE. Yes, sir, born at Brussels.

GIBBET. A Frenchman, and a priest! I won't be seen in his company, sir; I have a value for my reputation, sir.

AIMWELL. Nay, but Captain, since we are by our selves – Can he speak English, landlord?

BONNIFACE. Very well, sir, you may know him, as the saying is, to be a foreigner by his accent, and that's all.

AIMWELL. Then he has been in England before?

BONNIFACE. Never, sir, but he's a master of languages, as the saying is, he talks Latin, it do's me good to hear him talk Latin.

AIMWELL. Then you understand Latin, Mr. Bonniface?

BONNIFACE. Not I, sir, as the saying is, but he talks it so very fast that I'm sure it must be good.

AIMWELL. Pray desire him to walk up.

BONNIFACE. Here he is, as the saying is.

Enter FOIGARD.

FOIGARD. Save you, gentlemen's, both.

AIMWELL. A Frenchman! Sir, your most humble servant.

FOIGARD. Och, dear joy, I am your most faithful shervant, and yours alsho.

GIBBET. Doctor, you talk very good English, but you have a mighty twang of the foreigner.

FOIGARD. My English is very vel for the vords, but we foreigners you know cannot bring our tongues about the pronunciation so soon.

AIMWELL. A foreigner! a down-right teague by this light. (*Aside.*) Were you born in France, Doctor?

FOIGARD. I was educated in France, but I was borned at Brussels, I am a subject of the King of Spain, joy.

GIBBET. What King of Spain, sir, speak.

FOIGARD. Upon my shoul joy, I cannot tell you as yet.

AIMWELL. Nay, captain, that was too hard upon the Doctor, he's a stranger.

FOIGARD. O let him alone, dear joy, I am of a nation that is not easily put out of countenance.

AIMWELL. Come, gentlemen, I'll end the dispute. – Here, landlord, is dinner ready?

BONNIFACE. Upon the table, as the saying is.

AIMWELL. Gentlemen – pray – that door–

FOIGARD. No, no fait, the captain must lead.

AIMWELL. No, Doctor, the Church is our guide.

GIBBET. Ay, ay, so it is. –

Exit foremost, they follow.

[Act III, Scene iii]

Scene changes to a gallery in LADY BOUNTIFUL'*s house. Enter* ARCHER *and* SCRUB *singing, and hugging one another,* SCRUB *with a tankard in his hand,* GIPSEY *listening at a distance.*

SCRUB. *Tall, all dall* – Come, my dear boy – Let's have that song once more.

ARCHER. No, no, we shall disturb the family; – But will you be sure to keep the secret?

SCRUB. Pho! upon my honour, as I'm a gentleman.

ARCHER. 'Tis enough. – You must know then that my master is the Lord Viscount Aimwell; he fought a duel t'other day in London, wounded his man so dangerously, that he thinks fit to withdraw till he hears whether the gentleman's wounds be mortal or not: He never was in this part of England before, so he chose to retire to this place, that's all.

GIPSEY. And that's enough for me.

Exit.

SCRUB. And where were you when your master fought?

ARCHER. We never know of our masters' quarrels.

SCRUB. No! if our masters in the country here receive a challenge, the first thing they do is to tell their wives; the wife tells the servants, the servants alarm the tenants, and in half an hour you shall have the whole county in arms.

ARCHER. To hinder two men from doing what they have no mind for: – But if you should chance to talk now of my business?

SCRUB. Talk! ay, sir, had I not learned the knack of holding my tongue, I had never liv'd so long in a great family.

ARCHER. Ay, ay, to be sure there are secrets in all families.

SCRUB. Secrets, ay; – But I'll say no more. – Come, sit down, we'll make an end of our tankard: Here –

ARCHER. With all my heart; who knows but you and I may come to be better acquainted, eh – Here's your ladies' healths; you have three, I think, and to be sure there must be secrets among 'em.

SCRUB. Secrets! Ay, friend; I wish I had a friend –

ARCHER. Am not I your friend? come, you and I will be sworn brothers.

SCRUB. Shall we?

ARCHER. From this minute. – Give me a kiss – And now brother
Scrub –

SCRUB. And now, brother Martin, I will tell you a secret that will
make your hair stand on end: You must know, that I am consumedly in love.

ARCHER. That's a terrible secret, that's the truth on't.

SCRUB. That jade, Gipsey, that was with us just now in the cellar,
is the arrantest whore that ever wore a petticoat; and I'm dying
for love of her.

ARCHER. Ha, ha, ha – Are you in love with her Person, or her
vertue, brother Scrub?

SCRUB. I should like vertue best, because it is more durable than
beauty; for vertue holds good with some women long, and many a
day after they have lost it.

ARCHER. In the country, I grant ye, where no woman's vertue is
lost, till a bastard be found.

SCRUB. Ay, could I bring her to a bastard, I should have her all to
myself; but I dare not put it upon that lay, for fear of being sent
for a soldier. – Pray, brother, how do you gentlemen in London
like that same Pressing Act?

ARCHER. Very ill, brother Scrub; – 'tis the worst that ever was
made for us: Formerly I remember the good days, when we could
dun our masters for our wages, and if they refused to pay us, we
could have a warrant to carry 'em before a Justice; but now if we
talk of eating, they have a warrant for us, and carry us before
three Justices.

SCRUB. And to be sure we go, if we talk of eating; for the Justices
won't give their own servants a bad example. Now this is my
misfortune dare not speak in the house, while that jade Gipsey
dings about like a fury – Once I had the better end of the staff.

ARCHER. And how comes the change now?

SCRUB. Why, the mother of all this mischief is a priest.

ARCHER. A priest!

SCRUB. Ay, a damn'd son of a whore of Babylon, that came over hither to say grace to the French officers, and eat up our provisions – There's not a day goes over his head without dinner or supper in this house.

ARCHER. How came he so familiar in the family?

SCRUB. Because he speaks English as if he had liv'd here all his life; and tells lies as if he had been a traveller from his cradle.

ARCHER. And this priest, I'm afraid has converted the affections of your Gipsey.

SCRUB. Converted! ay, and perverted, my dear friend: – For I'm afraid he has made her a whore and a Papist. – But this is not all; there's the French Count and Mrs. Sullen, they're in the confederacy, and for some private ends of their own to be sure.

ARCHER. A very hopeful family yours, brother Scrub; I suppose the maiden lady has her lover too.

SCRUB. Not that I know; – She's the best on 'em, that's the truth on't: But they take care to prevent my curiosity, by giving me so much business, that I'm a perfect slave. – What d'ye think is my place in this family?

ARCHER. Butler, I suppose.

SCRUB. Ah, Lord help you – I'll tell you – Of a Monday, I drive the coach; of a Tuesday, I drive the plough; on Wednesday, I follow the hounds; a Thursday, I dun the tenants; on Friday, I go to market; on Saturday, I draw warrants; and a Sunday, I draw beer.

ARCHER. Ha, ha, ha! if variety be a pleasure in life, you have enough on't, my dear brother – But what ladies are those?

SCRUB. Ours, ours; that upon the right hand is Mrs. Sullen, and the other is Mrs. Dorinda. – Don't mind 'em, sit still, man –

Enter MRS SULLEN, *and* DORINDA.

MRS SULLEN. I have heard my brother talk of my Lord Aimwell,
but they say that his brother is the finer gentleman.

DORINDA. That's impossible, sister.

MRS SULLEN. He's vastly rich, but very close, they say.

DORINDA. No matter for that; if I can creép into his heart, I'll
open his breast, warrant him: I have heard say, that people may
be guess'd at by the behaviour of their servants; I could wish we
might talk to that fellow.

MRS SULLEN. So do I; for, I think he's a very pretty fellow: Come
this way, I'll throw out a lure for him presently.

They walk a turn towards the opposite side of the stage, MRS SULLEN
drops her glove, ARCHER *runs, takes it up, and gives it to her.*

ARCHER. Corn, wine, and oil, indeed – But, I think, the wife has
the greatest plenty of flesh and blood; she should be my choice –
Ah, a, say you so – madam – your ladyship's glove.

MRS SULLEN. O, sir, I thank you – what a handsome bow the
fellow has?

DORINDA. Bow! why I have known several footmen come down
from London, set up here for dancing-masters, and carry off the
best fortunes in the country.

ARCHER (*aside*). That project, for ought I know, had been better
than ours. Brother Scrub – Why don't you introduce me.

SCRUB. Ladies, this is the strange gentleman's servant that you
see at church today; I understood he came from London, and so
I invited him to the cellar, that he might show me the newest
flourish in whetting my knives.

DORINDA. And I hope you have made much of him?

ARCHER. O yes, madam, but the strength of your ladyship's
liquor is a little too potent for the constitution of your humble
servant.

MRS SULLEN. What, then you don't usually drink ale?

ARCHER. No, madam, my constant drink is tea, or a little wine and
water; 'tis prescrib'd me by the physician for a remedy against the
spleen.

SCRUB. O la, O la! a footman have the spleen. –

MRS SULLEN. I thought that distemper had been only proper to
people of quality.

ARCHER. Madam, like all other fashions it wears out, and so
descends to their servants; though in a great many of us, I believe
it proceeds from some melancholy particles in the blood,
occasion'd by the stagnation of wages.

DORINDA. How affectedly the fellow talks – How long, pray, have
you serv'd your present master?

ARCHER. Not long; my life has been mostly spent in the service of
the ladies.

MRS SULLEN. And pray, which service do you like best?

ARCHER. Madam, the ladies pay best; the honour of serving them
is sufficient wages; there is a charm in their looks that delivers a
pleasure with their commands, and gives our duty the wings of
inclination.

MRS SULLEN. That flight was above the pitch of a livery; and, sir,
would not you be satisfied to serve a lady again?

ARCHER. As a groom of the chamber, Madam, but not as a
footman.

MRS SULLEN. I suppose you serv'd as footman before.

ARCHER. For that reason I would not serve in that post again; for
my memory is too weak for the load of messages that the ladies
lay upon their servants in London; my Lady Howd'ye, the last
mistress I serv'd call'd me up one morning, and told me, Martin,
go to my Lady Allnight with my humble service; tell her I was to
wait on her Ladyship yesterday, and left word with Mrs Rebecca,
that the preliminaries of the affair she knows of, are stopped till
we know the concurrence of the person that I know of, for which
there are circumstances wanting which we shall accommodate

at the old place; but that in the meantime there is a person about her Ladyship, that from several hints and surmises, was accessory at a certain time to the disappointments that naturally attend things, that to her knowledge are of more importance.

MRS SULLEN [and] DORINDA. Ha, ha. ha! where are you going, sir?

ARCHER. Why, I han't half done. – The whole Howd'ye was about half an hour long; so I happened to misplace two syllables, and was turn'd off, and render'd incapable –

DORINDA. The pleasantest fellow, sister, I ever saw. – But, friend, if your master be married, – I presume you still serve a lady.

ARCHER. No, madam, I take care never to come into a married family; the commands of the master and mistress are always so contrary, that 'tis impossible to please both.

DORINDA. There's a main point gain'd. – My Lord is not married, I find. (*Aside.*)

MRS SULLEN. But, I wonder, friend, that in so many good services, you had not a better provision made for you.

ARCHER. I don't know how, madam. I had a lieutenancy offer'd me three or four times; but that is not bread, madam – I live much better as I do.

SCRUB. Madam, he sings rarely. – I was thought to do pretty well here in the country till he came; but alack a day, I'm nothing to my brother Martin.

DORINDA. Does he? Pray, sir, will you oblige us with a song?

ARCHER. Are you for passion, or humour?

SCRUB. O le! he has the purest ballad about a trifle –

MRS SULLEN. A trifle! pray, sir, let's have it.

ARCHER. I'm asham'd to offer you a trifle, madam: But since you command me –

(Sings to the tune of Sir Simon the King.)

A trifling song you shall hear,
Begun with a trifle and ended:
All trifling people draw near,
And I shall be nobly attended.

Were it not for trifles, a few,
That lately have come into play;
The men would want something to do,
And the women want something to say.

What makes men trifle in dressing?
Because the ladies (they know)
Admire, by often possessing,
That eminent trifle a beau.

When the lover his moments has trifled,
The trifle of trifles to gain:
No sooner the virgin is rifled,
But a trifle shall part 'em again.

What mortal man would be able
At White's half an hour to sit?
Or who could bear a tea-table,
Without talking of trifles for wit?

The Court is from trifles secure,
Gold keys are no trifles, we see:
White rods are no trifles, I'm sure,
Whatever their bearers may be.

But if you will go to the place,
Where trifles abundantly breed,
The levee will show you his Grace
Makes promises trifles indeed.

A coach with six footmen behind,
I count neither trifle nor sin:
But, ye Gods! how oft do we find
A scandalous trifle within?

A flask of champagne, people think it
A trifle, or something as bad:
But if you'll contrive how to drink it,
You'll find it no trifle egad.

A parson's a trifle at sea,
A widow's a trifle in sorrow:
A peace is a trifle today,
Who knows what may happen tomorrow?

A black coat, a trifle may cloak,
Or to hide it, the red may endeavour:
But if once the army is broke,
We shall have more trifles than ever.

The stage is a trifle, they say,
The reason, pray carry along,
Because at ev'ry new play,
The house they with trifles so throng.

But with people's malice to trifle,
And to set us all on a foot:
The author of this is a trifle,
And his song is a trifle to boot.

MRS SULLEN. Very well, sir, we're obliged to you. – Something
for a pair of gloves.

Offering him money.

ARCHER. I humbly beg leave to be excused: My master, Madam,
pays me; nor dare I take money from any other hand without
injuring his honour, and disobeying his commands.

Exit.

DORINDA. This is surprising: Did you ever see so pretty a well bred
fellow?

MRS SULLEN. The Devil take him for wearing that livery.

DORINDA. I fancy, sister, he may be some gentleman, a friend
of my Lord's, that his Lordship has pitch'd upon for his courage,
fidelity, and discretion to bear him company in this dress, and
who, ten to one was his second too.

MRS SULLEN. It is so, it must be so, and it shall be so: – For I like him.

DORINDA. What! better than the Count?

MRS SULLEN. The Count happen'd to be the most agreeable man upon the place; and so I chose him to serve me in my design upon my husband. – But I should like this fellow better in a design upon my self.

DORINDA. But now, sister, for an interview with this Lord, and this gentleman; how shall we bring that about?

MRS SULLEN. Patience! you country ladies give no quarter, if once you be enter'd. – Would you prevent their desires, and give the fellows no wishing-time? – Look'ye, Dorinda, if my Lord Aimwell loves you or deserves you, he'll find a way to see you, and there we must leave it. – My business comes now upon the tapis – Have you prepar'd your brother?

DORINDA. Yes, yes.

MRS SULLEN. And how did he relish it?

DORINDA. He said little, mumbled something to himself, promis'd to be guided by me: But here he comes –

Enter SULLEN.

SULLEN. What singing was that I heard just now?

MRS SULLEN. The singing in your head, my dear, you complain'd of it all day.

SULLEN. You're impertinent.

MRS SULLEN. I was ever so, since I became one flesh with you.

SULLEN. One flesh! rather two carcasses join'd unnaturally together.

MRS SULLEN. Or rather a living soul coupled to a dead body.

DORINDA. So, this is fine encouragement for me.

SULLEN. Yes, my wife shows you what you must do.

MRS SULLEN. And my husband shows you what you must suffer.

SULLEN. S'death, why can't you be silent?

MRS SULLEN. S'death, why can't you talk?

SULLEN. Do you talk to any purpose?

MRS SULLEN. Do you think to any purpose?

SULLEN. Sister, heark'ye; (*Whispers.*) I shan't be home till it be late.

   Exit.

MRS SULLEN. What did he whisper to ye?

DORINDA. That he would go round the back way, come into the closet, and listen as I directed him. – But let me beg you once more, dear sister, to drop this project; for, as I told you before, instead of awaking him to kindness, you may provoke him to a rage; and then who knows how far his brutality may carry him?

MRS SULLEN. I'm provided to receive him, I warrant you: But here comes the Count, vanish.

   Exit DORINDA. *Enter* COUNT BELLAIR.

Don't you wonder, Monsieur le Count, that I was not at church this afternoon?

COUNT. I more wonder, madam, that you go dere at all, or how you dare to lift those eyes to heaven that are guilty of so much killing.

MRS SULLEN. If Heaven, sir, has given to my eyes with the power of killing, the virtue of making a cure, I hope the one may atone for the other.

COUNT. O largely, madam; would your Ladyship be as ready to apply the remedy as to give the wound? – Consider, madam, I am doubly a prisoner; first to the arms of your general, then to your more conquering eyes; my first chains are easy, there a ransom may redeem me, but from your fetters I never shall get free.

MRS SULLEN. Alas, sir, why should you complain to me of your captivity, who am in chains myself? you know, sir, that I am bound, nay, must be tied up in that particular that might give you ease: I am like you, a prisoner of war – of war indeed: – I have given my parole of honour; would you break yours to gain your liberty?

COUNT. Most certainly I would, were I a prisoner among the Turks; dis is your case; you're a slave, madam, slave to the worst of Turks, a husband.

MRS SULLEN. There lies my foible, I confess; no fortifications, no courage, conduct, nor vigilancy can pretend to defend a place, where the cruelty of the governor forces the garrison to mutiny.

COUNT. And where de besieger is resolv'd to die before de place – Here will I fix; (*Kneels.*) with tears, vows, and prayers assault your heart, and never rise till you surrender; or if I must storm – love and St. Michael – And so I begin the attack –

MRS SULLEN. Stand off – Sure he hears me not – And I could almost wish he – did not. – The fellow makes love very prettily. (*Aside.*) But, sir, why should you put such a value upon my person, when you see it despis'd by one that knows it so much better.

COUNT. He knows it not, though he possesses it; if he but knew the value of the jewel he is master of, he would always wear it next his heart, and sleep with it in his arms.

MRS SULLEN. But since he throws me unregarded from him.

COUNT. And one that knows your value well, comes by, and takes you up, is it not justice.

Goes to lay hold on her. Enter SULLEN with his sword drawn.

SULLEN. Hold, villain, hold.

MRS SULLEN (*presenting a pistol*). Do you hold.

SULLEN. What! Murther your husband, to defend your bully.

MRS SULLEN. Bully! for shame, Mr. Sullen; Bullies wear long swords, the gentleman has none, he's a prisoner you know – I was aware of your outrage, and prepar'd this to receive your violence, and, if occasion were, to preserve my self against the force of this other gentleman.

COUNT. O madam, your eyes be bettre firearms than your pistol, they nevre miss.

SULLEN. What! court my wife to my face!

MRS SULLEN. Pray, Mr. Sullen, put up, suspend your fury for a minute.

SULLEN. To give you time to invent an excuse.

MRS SULLEN. I need none.

SULLEN. No, for I heard every syllable of your discourse.

COUNT. Ay! and begar, I tink de dialogue was vera pretty.

MRS SULLEN. Then I suppose, sir, you heard something of your own barbarity.

SULLEN. Barbarity! oons what does the woman call barbarity? do I ever meddle with you?

MRS SULLEN. No.

SULLEN. As for you, sir, I shall take another time.

COUNT. Ah, begar, and so must I.

SULLEN. Look'ee, madam, don't think that my anger proceeds from any concern I have for your honour, but for my own, and if you can contrive any way of being a whore without making me a cuckold, do it and welcome.

MRS SULLEN. Sir, I thank you kindly, you would allow me the sin but rob me of the pleasure – No, no, I'm resolv'd never to venture upon the crime without the satisfaction of seeing you punish'd for't.

SULLEN. Then will you grant me this, my dear? let any body else do you the favour but that Frenchman, for I mortally hate his whole generation.

Exit.

COUNT. Ah, sir, that be ungrateful, for begar, I love some of yours, Madam. – (*Approaching her.*)

MRS SULLEN. No, sir. –

COUNT. No, sir, – Garzoon, madam, I am not your husband.

MRS SULLEN. 'Tis time to undeceive you, sir, – I believ'd your addresses to me were no more than an amusement, and I hope you will think the same of my complaisance, and to convince you that you ought, you must know, that I brought you hither only to make you instrumental in setting me right with my husband, for he was planted to listen by my appointment.

COUNT. By your appointment?

MRS. SULLEN. Certainly.

COUNT. And so, madam, while I was telling twenty stories to part you from your husband, begar, I was bringing you together all the while.

MRS SULLEN. I ask your pardon, sir, but I hope this will give you a taste of the vertue of the English ladies.

COUNT. Begar, madam, your vertue be vera great, but garzoon your honeste be vera little.

Enter DORINDA.

MRS SULLEN. Nay, now you're angry, sir.

COUNT. Angry! fair *Dorinda* –

(*Sings* Dorinda *the Opera Tune, and addresses to Dorinda.*)

Madam, when your ladyship want a fool, send for me,

Fair Dorinda, revenge, etc.

Exit.

MRS SULLEN. There goes the true humour of his nation, resentment with good manners, and the height of anger in a song. – well sister, you must be judge, for you have heard the trial.

DORINDA. And I bring in my brother guilty.

MRS SULLEN. But I must bear the punishment, – 'Tis hard sister.

DORINDA. I own it – but you must have patience.

MRS SULLEN. Patience! the cant of custom – Providence sends no evil without a remedy – should I lie groaning under a yoke I can shake off, I were accessory to my ruin, and my patience were no better than self-murder.

DORINDA. But how can you shake off the yoke? – Your divisions don't come within the reach of the law for a divorce.

MRS SULLEN. Law! what law can search into the remote abyss of Nature, what evidence can prove the unaccountable disaffections of wedlock? – can a jury sum up the endless aversions that are rooted in our souls, or can a bench give judgment upon antipathies?

DORINDA. They never pretended sister, they never meddle but in case of uncleanness.

MRS SULLEN. Uncleanness! Sister, casual violation is a transient injury, and may possibly be repair'd, but can radical hatreds be ever reconcil'd – No, no, sister, Nature is the first lawgiver, and when she has set tempers opposite, not all the golden links of wedlock, nor iron manacles of law can keep 'um fast.

Wedlock we own ordain'd by Heaven's decree,
But such as Heaven ordain'd it first to be,
Concurring tempers in the man and wife
As mutual helps to draw the load of life.
View all the works of Providence above,
The stars with harmony and concord move;
View all the works of Providence below,
The fire, the water, earth, and air, we know
All in one plant agree to make it grow.
Must man the chiefest work of art divine,
Be doom'd in endless discord to repine.
No, we should injure heaven by that surmise,
Omnipotence is just, were man but wise.

End of the Third Act.

Act IV

Scene continues. Enter MRS. SULLEN.

MRS SULLEN. Were I born an humble Turk, where women have no soul nor property there I must sit contented – But in England, a country whose women are its glory, must women be abus'd, where women rule, must women be enslav'd? nay, cheated into slavery, mock'd by a promise of comfortable society into a wilderness of solitude – I dare not keep the thought about me, – O, here comes something to divert me –

Enter a COUNTRY WOMAN.

WOMAN. I come an't please your Ladyships, you're my Lady Bountiful an't ye?

MRS SULLEN. Well, good woman go on.

WOMAN. I come seventeen long mail to have a cure for my husband's sore leg.

MRS SULLEN. Your husband! what woman, cure your husband!

WOMAN. Ay, poor man, for his sore leg won't let him stir from home.

MRS SULLEN. There, I confess, you have given me a reason. Well good woman, I'll tell you what you must do – You must lay your husband's leg upon a table, and with a choping-knife, you must lay it open as broad as you can, then you must take out the bone, and beat the flesh soundly with a rowling-pin, then take salt, pepper, cloves, mace and ginger, some sweet herbs, and season it very well, then rowl it up like brawn, and put it into the oven for two hours.

WOMAN. Heavens reward your ladyship – I have two little babies too that are pitious bad with the graips, an't please ye.

MRS SULLEN. Put a little pepper and salt in their bellies, good woman.

Enter LADY BOUNTIFUL.

I beg your Ladyship's pardon for taking your business out of your hands, I have been a tampering here a little with one of your patients.

LADY BOUNTIFUL. Come, good woman, don't mind this mad creature, I am the person that you want, I suppose – What would you have, woman?

MRS SULLEN. She wants something for her husband's sore leg.

LADY BOUNTIFUL. What's the matter with his leg, Goody?

WOMAN. It come first as one might say with a sort of dizziness in his foot, then he had a kind of a laziness in his joints, and then his leg broke out, and then it swell'd, and then it clos'd again, and then it broke out again, and then it fester'd, and then it grew better, and then it grew worse again.

MRS SULLEN. Ha, ha, ha.

LADY BOUNTIFUL. How can you be merry with the misfortunes of other people?

MRS SULLEN. Because my own make me sad, madam.

LADY BOUNTIFUL. The worst reason in the world, daughter, your own misfortunes should teach you to pity others.

MRS SULLEN. But the woman's misfortunes and mine are nothing alike, her husband is sick, and mine, alas, is in health.

LADY BOUNTIFUL. What! would you wish your husband sick?

MRS SULLEN. Not of a sore leg, of all things.

LADY BOUNTIFUL. Well, good woman, go to the pantry, get your bellyfull of victuals, then I'll give you a receipt of diet-drink for your husband – But d'ye hear Goody, you must not let your husband move too much.

WOMAN. No, no, madam, the poor man's inclinable enough to lie still.

Exit.

LADY BOUNTIFUL. Well, daughter Sullen, though you laugh, I have done miracles about the country here with my receipts.

MRS SULLEN. Miracles, indeed, if they have cur'd anybody, but, I believe, madam, the patient's faith goes farther toward the miracle than your prescription.

LADY BOUNTIFUL. Fancy helps in some cases, but there's your husband who has as little fancy as any body, I brought him from death's-door.

MRS SULLEN. I suppose, madam, you made him drink plentifully of ass's milk.

Enter DORINDA, *runs to* MRS SULLEN.

DORINDA. News, dear sister, news, news.

Enter ARCHER *running.*

ARCHER. Where, where is my Lady Bountiful – Pray which is the old lady of you three?

LADY BOUNTIFUL. I am.

ARCHER. O, madam, the fame of your Ladyship's charity, goodness, benevolence, skill and ability have drawn me hither to implore your Ladyship's help in behalf of my unfortunate master, who is this moment breathing his last.

LADY BOUNTIFUL. Your master! where is he?

ARCHER. At your gate, madam, drawn by the appearance of your handsome house to view it nearer, and walking up the avenue within five paces of the courtyard, he was taken ill of a sudden with a sort of I know not what, but down he fell, and there he lies.

LADY BOUNTIFUL. Here, Scrub, Gipsey, all run, get my easy chair down stairs, put the gentleman in it, and bring him in quickly, quickly.

ARCHER. Heaven will reward your Ladyship for this charitable act.

LADY BOUNTIFUL. Is your master us'd to these fits?

ARCHER. O yes, madam, frequently – I have known him have five or six of a night.

LADY BOUNTIFUL. What's his name?

ARCHER. Lord, madam, he's a dying, a minute's care or neglect may save or destroy his life.

LADY BOUNTIFUL. Ah, poor gentleman! come friend, show me the way, I'll see him brought in myself.

Exit with ARCHER.

DORINDA. O sister my heart flutters about strangely, I can hardly forbear running to his assistance.

MRS SULLEN. And I'll lay my life, he deserves your assistance more than he wants it; did not I tell you that my Lord would find a way to come at you. Love's his distemper, and you must be the physician; put on all your charms, summon all your fire into your eyes, plant the whole artillery of your looks against his breast, and down with him.

DORINDA. O sister, I'm but a young gunner, I shall be afraid to shoot, for fear the piece should recoil and hurt my self.

MRS SULLEN. Never fear, you shall see me shoot before you, if you will.

DORINDA. No, no, dear sister, you have miss'd your mark so unfortunately, that I shan't care for being instructed by you.

Enter AIMWELL *in a chair, carried by* ARCHER *and* SCRUB, LADY BOUNTIFUL, GIPSEY. AIMWELL *counterfeiting a swoon.*

LADY BOUNTIFUL. Here, here, let's see the hartshorn drops – Gipsey a glass of fair water, his fit's very strong – Bless me, how his hands are clench'd.

ARCHER. For shame, ladies, what d'ye do? why don't you help us – Pray, madam, (*To* DORINDA.) Take his hand and open it if you can, whilst I hold his head.

DORINDA *takes his Hand*.

DORINDA. Poor gentleman, – Oh – he has got my hand within his, and squeezes it unmercifully –

LADY BOUNTIFUL. 'Tis the violence of his convulsion, child.

ARCHER. O, madam, he's perfectly possess'd in these cases – he'll bite if you don't have a care.

DORINDA. Oh, my hand, my hand.

LADY BOUNTIFUL. What's the matter with the foolish girl? I have got this hand open, you see, with a great deal of ease.

ARCHER. Ay, but, madam, your daughter's hand is somewhat warmer than your Ladyship's, and the heat of it draws the force of the spirits that way.

MRS SULLEN. I find, friend, you're very learned in these sorts of fits.

ARCHER. 'Tis no wonder, madam, for I'm often troubled with them my self, I find my self extremely ill at this minute. (*Looking hard at* MRS SULLEN.)

MRS SULLEN (*aside*). I fancy I could find a way to cure you.

LADY BOUNTIFUL. His fit holds him very long.

ARCHER. Longer than usual, madam, – Pray, young lady, open his breast, and give him air.

LADY BOUNTIFUL. Where did his illness take him first, pray?

ARCHER. Today at church, madam.

LADY BOUNTIFUL. In what manner was he taken?

ARCHER. Very strangely, my lady. He was of a sudden touch'd with something in his eyes, which at the first he only felt, but could not tell whether 'twas pain or pleasure.

LADY BOUNTIFUL. Wind, nothing but wind.

ARCHER. By soft degrees it grew and mounted to his brain, there his fancy caught it; there form'd it so beautiful, and dress'd it up

in such gay pleasing colours, that his transported appetite
seiz'd the fair idea, and straight convey'd it to his heart. That
hospitable seat of life sent all its sanguine spirits forth to meet,
and open'd all its sluicy gates to take the stranger in.

LADY BOUNTIFUL. Your master should never go without a bottle
to smell to – Oh! – He recovers – The lavender water – Some
feathers to burn under his nose – Hungary-water to rub his
temples – O, he comes to himself. Hem a little, sir, hem –
Gipsey, bring the cordial-water.

AIMWELL *seems to awake in amaze.*

DORINDA. How d'ye, sir?

AIMWELL. Where am I? (*Rising.*)

Sure I have pass'd the gulf of silent death,
And now I land on the Elysian shore–
Behold the goddess of those happy plains,
Fair Proserpine – Let me adore thy bright divinity.

Kneels to DORINDA *and kisses her hand.*

MRS SULLEN. So, so, so, I knew where the fit would end.

AIMWELL. Euridice perhaps –

How could thy Orpheus keep his word,
And not look back upon thee;
No treasure but thyself could sure have brib'd him
To look one minute off thee.

LADY BOUNTIFUL. Delirious, poor gentleman.

ARCHER. Very delirious, madam, very delirious.

AIMWELL. Martin's voice, I think.

ARCHER. Yes, my Lord – How do's your Lordship?

LADY BOUNTIFUL. Lord! did you mind that, girls.

AIMWELL. Where am I?

ARCHER. In very good hands, sir, – You were taken just now
with one of your old fits under the trees just by this good lady's

house, her Ladyship had you taken in, and has miraculously brought you to your self, as you see –

AIMWELL. I am so confounded with shame, madam, that I can now only beg pardon – And refer my acknowledgements for your Ladyship's care, till an opportunity offers of making some amends – I dare be no longer troublesome – Martin, give two guineas to the servants. (*Going.*)

DORINDA. Sir, you may catch cold by going so soon into the air, you don't look, sir, as if you were perfectly recover'd.

Here ARCHER *talks to* LADY BOUNTIFUL *in dumb show.*

AIMWELL. That I shall never be, madam, my present illness is so rooted, that I must expect to carry it to my grave.

MRS SULLEN. Don't despair, sir, I have known several in your distemper shake it off, with a fortnight's physic.

LADY BOUNTIFUL. Come, sir, your servant has been telling me that you're apt to relapse if you go into the air – Your good manners shan't get the better of ours – You shall sit down again, sir, – Come, sir, we don't mind ceremonies in the country – Here, sir, my service t'ye – You shall taste my water; 'tis a cordial I can assure you, and of my own making – drink it off, sir.

AIMWELL *drinks.*

And how d'ye find your self now, sir?

AIMWELL. Somewhat better – Though very faint still.

LADY BOUNTIFUL. Ay, ay, People are always faint after these fits – Come girls, you shall show the gentleman the house, 'tis but an old family building, sir, but you had better walk about and cool by degrees than venture immediately into the air – You'll find some tolerable pictures – Dorinda, show the gentleman the way. I must go to the poor woman below.

Exit.

DORINDA. This way, sir.

AIMWELL. Ladies shall I beg leave for my servant to wait on you, for he understands pictures very well.

MRS SULLEN. Sir, we understand originals, as well as he do's pictures, so he may come along.

Exeunt DORINDA, MRS SULLEN, AIMWELL, ARCHER. AIMWELL *leads* DORINDA.

Enter FOIGARD *and* SCRUB, *meeting.*

FOIGARD. Save you, Master Scrub.

SCRUB. Sir, I won't be sav'd your way – I hate a priest, I abhor the French, and I defy the Devil – Sir, I'm a bold Briton, and will spill the last drop of my blood to keep out popery and slavery.

FOIGARD. Master Scrub, you would put me down in politics, and so I would be speaking with Mrs. Shipsey.

SCRUB. Good Mr. Priest, you can't speak with her, she's sick, sir, she's gone abroad, sir, she's – dead two months ago, sir.

Enter GIPSEY.

GIPSEY. How now, impudence; how dare you talk so saucily to the Doctor? Pray, sir, don't take it ill; for the common people of England are not so civil to strangers, as –

SCRUB. You lie, you lie – 'Tis the common people that are civillest to strangers.

GIPSEY. Sirrah, I have a good mind to – Get you out, I say.

SCRUB. I won't.

GIPSEY. You won't, sauce-box – Pray, Doctor, what is the Captain's name that came to your inn last night?

SCRUB. The Captain! Ah, the Devil, there she hampers me again; – The Captain has me on one side, and the priest on t'other: – So between the gown and the sword, I have a fine time on't. – But, *Cedunt arma togae*. (*Going.*)

GIPSEY. What, sirrah, won't you march?

SCRUB. No, my dear, I won't march – But I'll walk – And I'll make bold to listen a little too.

Goes behind the side-scene, and listens.

GIPSEY. Indeed, Doctor, the Count has been barbarously treated, that's the truth on't.

FOIGARD. Ah, Mrs. Gipsey, upon my shoul, now, gra, his complainings would mollify the marrow in your bones, and move the bowels of your commiseration; he veeps, and he dances, and he fistles, and he swears, and he laughs, and he stamps, and he sings: In conclusion, joy, he's afflicted, *a la francois*, and a stranger would not know whider to cry, or to laugh with him.

GIPSEY. What would you have me do, Doctor?

FOIGARD. Noting, joy, but only hide the Count in Mrs. Sullen's closet when it is dark.

GIPSEY. Nothing! Is that nothing? it would be both a sin and a shame, Doctor.

FOIGARD. Here is twenty Lewidores, joy, for your shame; and I will give you an absolution for the shin.

GIPSEY. But won't that money look like a bribe?

FOIGARD. Dat is according as you shall tauk it. – If you receive the money beforehand, 'twill be *logicè* a bribe; but if you stay till afterwards, 'twill be only a gratification.

GIPSEY. Well, Doctor, I'll take it *logicè*. But what must I do with my conscience, sir?

FOIGARD. Leave dat wid me, joy; I am your priest, gra; and your conscience is under my hands.

GIPSEY. But should I put the Count into the closet –

FOIGARD. Vel, is dere any shin for a man's being in a closhet; one may go to prayers in a closhet.

GIPSEY. But if the lady should come into her chamber, and go to bed?

FOIGARD. Vel, and is dere any shin in going to bed, joy?

GIPSEY. Ay, but if the parties should meet, Doctor?

FOIGARD. Vel den – The parties must be responsible. – Do you be after putting the Count in the closet; and leave the shins wid themselves. I will come with the Count to instruct you in your chamber. –

GIPSEY. Well, Doctor, your religion is so pure – methinks I'm so easy after an absolution, and can sin afresh with so much security, that I'm resolv'd to die a martyr to't. – Here's the key of the garden-door, come in the back way when 'tis late, – I'll be ready to receive you; but don't so much as whisper, only take hold of my hand, I'll lead you, and do you lead the Count, and follow me.

Exeunt. Enter SCRUB.

SCRUB. What witchcraft now have these two Imps of the Devil been a-hatching here? – There's twenty Lewidores, I heard that, and saw the purse: But I must give room to my betters.

Enter AIMWELL leading DORINDA, and making love in dumb show MRS SULLEN and ARCHER.

MRS SULLEN. Pray, sir, (*To ARCHER.*) how d'ye like that piece?

ARCHER. O, 'tis Leda. – You find, madam, how Jupiter comes disguis'd to make love –

MRS SULLEN. But what think you there of Alexander's battles?

ARCHER. We want only a Le Brun, Madam, to draw greater battles, and a greater general of our own. – The Danube, madam, would make a greater figure in a picture than the Granicus; and we have our Ramelies to match their Arbela.

MRS SULLEN. Pray, sir, what head is that in the corner there?

ARCHER. O, madam, 'tis poor Ovid in his exile.

MRS SULLEN. What was he banish'd for?

ARCHER. His ambitious love, madam. (*Bowing.*) His misfortune touches me.

MRS SULLEN. Was he successful in his amours?

ARCHER. There he has left us in the dark. – He was too much a gentleman to tell.

MRS. SULLEN. If he were secret, I pity him.

ARCHER. And if he were successful, I envy him.

MRS SULLEN. How d'ye like that Venus over the chimney?

ARCHER. Venus! I protest, madam, I took it for your picture; but now I look again, 'tis not handsome enough.

MRS SULLEN. Oh, what a charm is flattery! if you would see my picture, there it is, over that cabinet; How d'ye like it?

ARCHER. I must admire any thing, madam, that has the least resemblance of you – But, methinks, madam –

He looks at the picture and MRS. SULLEN *three or four times, by turns.*

Pray, madam, who drew it?

MRS SULLEN. A famous hand, sir.

Here AIMWELL *and* DORINDA *go off.*

ARCHER. A famous hand, madam – Your eyes, indeed, are featur'd there; but where's the sparkling moisture shining fluid, in which they swim. The picture indeed has your dimples; but where's the swarm of killing Cupids that should ambush there? the lips too are figur'd out; but where's the carnation dew, the pouting ripeness that tempts the taste in the original?

MRS SULLEN. Had it been my lot to have match'd with such a man!

ARCHER. Your breasts too, presumptuous man! what! paint Heaven! *Apropo*, madam, in the very next picture is Salmoneus, that was struck dead with lightning, for offering to imitate Jove's thunder; I hope you serv'd the painter so, madam?

MRS SULLEN. Had my eyes the power of thunder, they should employ their lightning better.

ARCHER. There's the finest bed in that room, madam, I suppose 'tis your ladyship's bed-chamber.

MRS SULLEN. And what then, sir?

ARCHER. I think the quilt is the richest that ever I saw: – I can't at this distance, madam, distinguish the figures of the embroidery; will you give me leave, madam –

MRS SULLEN. The Devil take his impudence. – Sure if I gave him an opportunity, he durst not offer it. – I have a great mind to try. – (*Going.*)

Returns.

S'death, what am I doing? – And alone too! – Sister, sister?

Runs out.

ARCHER. I'll follow her close – (*Going.*)

For where a French man durst attempt to storm,
A Briton sure may well the work perform.

Enter SCRUB.

SCRUB. Martin, brother Martin.

ARCHER. O, brother Scrub, I beg your pardon, I was not a-going; here's a guinea, my master order'd you.

SCRUB. A guinea, hi, hi, hi, a guinea! eh – by this light it is a guinea; but I suppose you expect one and twenty shillings in change.

ARCHER. Not at all; I have another for Gipsey.

SCRUB. A guinea for her! Faggot and fire for the witch. – Sir, give me that guinea, and I'll discover a plot.

ARCHER. A plot!

SCRUB. Ay, Sir, a plot, and a horrid plot. – First, it must be a plot because there's a woman in't; secondly, it must be a plot because there's a priest in't; thirdly, it must be a plot because there's French gold in't; and fourthly, it must be a plot, because I don't know what to make on't.

ARCHER. Nor any body else, I'm afraid, brother Scrub.

SCRUB. Truly I'm afraid so too; for where there's a priest and a woman, there's always a mystery and a riddle. – This I know, that here has been the doctor with a temptation in one hand, and an absolution in the other; and Gipsey has sold herself to the Devil; I saw the price paid down, my eyes shall take their oath on't.

ARCHER. And is all this bustle about Gipsey.

SCRUB. That's not all; I could hear but a word here and there; but I recall they mention'd a Count, a closet, a back door, and a key.

ARCHER. The Count! did you hear nothing of Mrs. Sullen?

SCRUB. I did hear some word that sounded that way; but whether it was Sullen or Dorinda, I could not distinguish.

ARCHER. You have told this matter to no body, brother?

SCRUB. Told! No, sir, I thank you for that; I'm resolv'd never to speak one word *pro* nor *con,* till we have a peace.

ARCHER. You're i'th right, brother Scrub; here's a treaty a foot between the Count and the lady. – The priest and the chambermaid are the plenipotentiaries. – It shall go hard but I find a way to be included in the treaty. – Where's the Doctor now?

SCRUB. He and Gipsey are this moment devouring my lady's marmalade in the closet.

AIMWELL *(from without)*. Martin, Martin.

ARCHER. I come, sir, I come.

SCRUB. But you forget the other guinea, brother Martin.

ARCHER. Here, I give it with all my heart.

SCRUB. And I take it with all my soul.

Exeunt severally.

I'cod, I'll spoil your plotting, Mrs. Gipsey; and if you should set the Captain upon me, these two guineas will buy me off.

Exit.

Enter MRS. SULLEN *and* DORINDA *meeting.*

MRS SULLEN. Well, sister.

DORINDA. And well, sister.

MRS SULLEN. What's become of my Lord?

DORINDA. What's become of his servant?

MRS SULLEN. Servant! he's a prettier fellow, and a finer gentleman by fifty degrees than his master.

DORINDA. O'my conscience, I fancy you could beg that fellow at the gallowsfoot.

MRS SULLEN. O'my conscience, I could, provided I could put a friend of yours in his room.

DORINDA. You desir'd me, sister to leave you, when you transgress'd the bounds of honour.

MRS SULLEN. Thou dear censorious country-girl – What dost mean? you can't think of the man without the bedfellow, I find.

DORINDA. I don't find any thing unnatural in that thought, while the mind is conversant with flesh and blood, it must conform to the humours of the company.

MRS SULLEN. How a little love and good company improves a woman; why, child, you begin to live – you never spoke before.

DORINDA. Because I was never spoke to. My Lord has told me that I have more wit and beauty than any of my sex; and truly I begin to think the man is sincere.

MRS SULLEN. You're in the right, Dorinda, pride is the life of a woman, and flattery is our daily bread; and she's a fool that won't believe a man there, as much as she that believes him in any thing else – But I'll lay you a guinea, that I had finer things said to me than you had.

DORINDA. Done – What did your fellow say to'ye?

MRS SULLEN. My fellow took the picture of Venus for mine.

DORINDA. But my lover took me for Venus herself.

MRS SULLEN. Common cant! had my spark call'd me a Venus directly, I should have believ'd him a footman in good earnest.

DORINDA. But my lover was upon his knees to me.

MRS SULLEN. And mine was upon his tiptoes to me.

DORINDA. Mine vow'd to die for me.

MRS SULLEN. Mine swore to die with me.

DORINDA. Mine spoke the softest moving things.

MRS SULLEN. Mine had his moving things too.

DORINDA. Mine kiss'd my hand ten thousand times.

MRS SULLEN. Mine has all that pleasure to come.

DORINDA. Mine offer'd marriage.

MRS SULLEN. O lard! D'ye call that a moving thing?

DORINDA. The sharpest arrow in his quiver, my dear sister, – why, my ten thousand pounds may lie brooding here this seven years, and hatch nothing at last but some ill natur'd clown like yours: – Whereas, If I marry my Lord Aimwell, there will be title, place and precedence, the park, the play, and the drawing-room, splendour, equipage, noise and flambeaux – Hey, my Lady Aimwell's servants there – Lights, lights to the stairs – My Lady Aimwell's coach put forward – Stand by, make room for her Ladyship – Are not these things moving? – What! melancholy of a sudden?

MRS SULLEN. Happy, happy sister! your angel has been watchful for your happiness, whilst mine has slept regardless of his charge. – Long smiling years of circling joys for you, but not one hour for me! (*Weeps.*)

DORINDA. Come, my dear, we'll talk of something else.

MRS SULLEN. O Dorinda, I own myself a woman, full of my sex, a gentle, generous soul, – easy and yielding to soft desires; a spacious heart, where love and all his train might lodge. And must the fair apartment of my breast be made a stable for a brute to lie in?

DORINDA. Meaning your husband, I suppose.

MRS SULLEN. Husband! no, – Even husband is too soft a name for
him. – But, come, I expect my brother here tonight or tomorrow;
he was abroad when my father married me; perhaps he'll find a
way to make me easy.

DORINDA. Will you promise not to make your self easy in the
mean time with my Lord's friend?

MRS SULLEN. You mistake me, sister – It happens with us, as
among the men, the greatest talkers are the greatest cowards; and
there's a reason for it; those spirits evaporate in prattle, which
might do more mischief if they took another course; – Though to
confess the truth, I do love that fellow; And if I met him dressed
as he should be, and I undressed as I should be – Look'ye, sister,
I have no supernatural gifts; – I can't swear I could resist the
temptation, – though I can safely promise to avoid it; and that's
as much as the best of us can do.

Exeunt MRS SULLEN *and* DORINDA.

Enter AIMWELL *and* ARCHER *laughing*.

ARCHER. And the awkward kindness of the good motherly old
gentlewoman –

AIMWELL. And the coming easiness of the young one – S'death, 'tis
pity to deceive her.

ARCHER. Nay, if you adhere to those principles, stop where you
are.

AIMWELL. I can't stop; for I love her to distraction.

ARCHER. S'death, if you love her a hair's breadth beyond discretion, you must go no farther.

AIMWELL. Well, well, any thing to deliver us from sauntering away
our idle evenings at White's, Tom's, or Will's, and be stinted to
bear looking at our old acquaintance, the cards; because our
impotent pockets can't afford us a guinea for the mercenary
drabs.

ARCHER. Or be oblig'd to some purse-proud coxcomb for a scandalous bottle, where we must not pretend to our share of the discourse, because we can't pay our club o'th reckoning; – damn it, I had rather sponge upon Morris, and sup upon a dish of Bohee scored behind the Door.

AIMWELL. And there expose our want of sense by talking criticisms, as we should our want of money by railing at the government.

ARCHER. Or be oblig'd to sneak into the side-box, and between both houses steal two acts of a play, and because we haven't money to see the other three, we come away discontented, and damn the whole five.

AIMWELL. And ten thousand such rascally tricks, – had we outliv'd our fortunes among our acquaintance. – But now –

ARCHER. Ay, now is the time to prevent all this. – Strike while the iron is hot. – This priest is the luckiest part of our adventure; He shall marry you, and pimp for me.

AIMWELL. But I should not like a woman that can be so fond of a Frenchman.

ARCHER. Alas, sir, necessity has no law; the lady may be in distress; perhaps she has a confounded husband, and her revenge may carry her farther than her love. – I'gad, I have so good an opinion of her, and of myself, that I begin to fancy strange things; and we must say this for the honour of our women, and indeed of ourselves, that they do stick to their men, as they do to their Magna Charta. – If the plot lies as I suspect, – I must put on the gentleman. – But here comes the Doctor. – I shall be ready.

Exit. Enter FOIGARD.

FOIGARD. Sauve you, noble friend.

AIMWELL. O sir, your servant; pray Doctor, may I crave your name?

FOIGARD. Fat naam is upon me? my Naam is Foigard, joy.

AIMWELL. Foigard, a very good name for a clergyman: Pray, Doctor Foigard, were you ever in Ireland?

FOIGARD. Ireland! No joy. – Fat sort of plaace is dat saam Ireland? dey say de people are catcht dere when dey are young.

AIMWELL. And some of 'em when they're old; – as for example.

Takes FOIGARD *by the shoulder.*

Sir, I arrest you as a traitor against the government; you're a subject of England, and this morning show'd me a commission, by which you serv'd as chaplain in the French army: This is death by our law, and your reverence must hang for't.

FOIGARD. Upon my shoul, noble friend, dis is strange news you tell me, Fader Foigard a subject of England, de son of a burgomaster of Brussels, a subject of England! Ubooboo –

AIMWELL. The son of a bogtrotter in Ireland; Sir, your tongue will condemn you before any Bench in the kingdom.

FOIGARD. And is my tongue all your evidensh, joy?

AIMWELL. That's enough.

FOIGARD. No, no, joy, for I vill never spake English no more.

AIMWELL. Sir, I have other evidence – Here, Martin, you know this fellow.

Enter ARCHER.

ARCHER (*in a brogue*). Saave you, my dear cussen, how do's your health?

FOIGARD. Ah! upon my shoul dere is my countryman, and his brogue will hang mine. (*Aside.*) *Mynheer, Ick wet neat watt hey zacht, Ick universton ewe neat, sacramant.*

AIMWELL. Altering your language won't do, sir, this fellow knows your person, and will swear to your face.

FOIGARD. Faace! fey, is dear a brogue upon my faash, too?

ARCHER. Upon my soulvation dere ish joy – But Cussen Mackshane vil you not put a remembrance upon me?

FOIGARD. Mack-shane! by St. Paatrick, dat is naame, shure enough. (*Aside.*)

AIMWELL. I fancy Archer, you have it.

FOIGARD. The Devil hang you, joy – By fat acquaintance are you my cussen.

ARCHER. O, de Devil hang your shelf, joy, you know we were little boys togeder upon de school, and your foster moder's son was married upon my nurse's chister, joy, and so we are Irish cussens.

FOIGARD. De Devil taak the relation! vel, joy, and fat school was it?

ARCHER. I tinks it vas – aay – 'twas Tipperary.

FOIGARD. No, no, joy, it vas Kilkenny.

AIMWELL. That's enough for us – self-confession – Come, sir, we must deliver you into the hands of the next magistrate.

ARCHER. He sends you to gaol, you're tried next assizes, and away you go swing into Purgatory.

FOIGARD. And is it so wid you, cussen?

ARCHER. It vil be sho wid you, cussen, if you don't immediately confess the secret between you and Mrs. Gipsey – Look'ee, sir, the gallows or the secret, take your choice.

FOIGARD. The gallows! upon my shoul I hate that saam gallow, for it is a diseash dat is fatal to our family – Vel den, dere is nothing, shentlemens, but Mrs. Shullen would spaak wid the Count in her chamber at midnight, and dere is no haarm, joy, for I am to conduct the Count to the plash, my shelf.

ARCHER. As I guess'd – Have you communicated the matter to the Count?

FOIGARD. I have not sheen him since.

ARCHER. Right agen; why then, Doctor – you shall conduct me to the lady instead of the Count.

FOIGARD. Fat my cussen to the lady! upon my shoul, gra, dat is too much upon the brogue.

ARCHER. Come, come, Doctor, consider we have got a rope about your neck, and if you offer to squeak, we'll stop your windpipe, most certainly, we shall have another job for you in a day or two, I hope.

AIMWELL. Here's company coming this way, let's into my chamber, and there concert our affair farther.

ARCHER. Come, my dear cussen, come along.

Exeunt. Enter BONNIFACE, HOUNSLOW *and* BAGSHOT *at one door*, GIBBET *at the opposite*.

GIBBET. Well, gentlemen, 'tis a fine night for our enterprise.

HOUNSLOW. Dark as hell.

BAGSHOT. And blows like the Devil; our landlord here has show'd us the window where we must break in, and tells us the plate stands in the wainscoat cupboard in the parlour.

BONNIFACE. Ay, ay, Mr. Bagshot, as the saying is, knives and forks, and cups, and cans, and tumblers, and tankards – There's one tankard, as the saying is, that's near upon as big as me, it was a present to the squire from his godmother, and smells of nutmeg and toast like an East India ship.

HOUNSLOW. Then you say we must divide at the stair-head?

BONNIFACE. Yes, Mr. Hounslow, as the saying is – At one end of that gallery lies my Lady Bountiful and her daughter, and at the other Mrs. Sullen – As for the Squire –

GIBBET. He's safe enough, I have fairly enter'd him, and he's more than half seas over already – But such a parcel of scoundrels are got about him now, that I gad I was asham'd to be seen in their company.

BONNIFACE. 'Tis now twelve, as the saying is – gentlemen, you must set out at one.

GIBBET. Hounslow, do you and Bagshot see our arms fix'd, and I'll come to you presently.

HOUNSLOW [and] BAGSHOT. We will.

Exeunt.

GIBBET. Well, my dear Bonny, you assure me that Scrub is a coward.

BONNIFACE. A chicken, as the saying is – You'll have no creature to deal with but the ladies.

GIBBET. And I can assure you, friend, there's a great deal of address and good manners in robbing a lady, I am the most a gentleman that way that ever travell'd the road – But, my dear Bonny, this prize will be a galleon, a Vigo business – I warrant you we shall bring off three or four thousand pound.

BONNIFACE. In plate, jewels and money, as the saying is, you may.

GIBBET. Why then, Tyburn, I defy thee, I'll get up to town, sell off my horse and arms, buy my self some pretty employment in the houshold, and be as snug, and as honest as any courtier of 'um all.

BONNIFACE. And what think you then of my daughter Cherry for a wife?

GIBBET. Look'ee, my dear Bonny – Cherry is the goddess I adore, as the song goes; but it is a maxim that man and wife should never have it in their power to hang one another, for if they should, the Lord have mercy on 'um both.

Exeunt.

End of the Fourth Act.

Act V

[Scene i]

Scene continues. Knocking without. Enter BONNIFACE.

BONNIFACE. Coming, coming – A coach and six foaming horses at this time o'night! Some great man, as the saying is, for he scorns to travel with other people.

Enter SIR CHARLES FREEMAN.

SIR CHARLES. What, fellow! a public-house, and abed when other people sleep.

BONNIFACE. Sir, I an't abed, as the saying is.

SIR CHARLES. Is Mr. Sullen's family, abed, think'ee?

BONNIFACE. All but the Squire himself, sir, as the saying is, he's in the house.

SIR CHARLES. What company has he?

BONNIFACE. Why, sir, there's the constable, Mr. Gage the exciseman, the hunchback'd barber, and two or three other gentlemen.

SIR CHARLES. I find my sister's letters gave me the true picture of her spouse.

Enter SULLEN *drunk.*

BONNIFACE. Sir, here's the Squire.

SULLEN. The puppies left me asleep – sir.

SIR CHARLES. Well, sir.

SULLEN. Sir, I'm an unfortunate man – I have three thousand pound a year, and I can't get a man to drink a cup of ale with me.

SIR CHARLES. That's very hard.

SULLEN. Ay, Sir – And unless you have pity upon me, and smoke one pipe with me, I must e'en go home to my wife, and I had rather go the Devil by half.

SIR CHARLES. But, I presume, sir, you won't see your wife tonight, she'll be gone to bed – you don't use to lie with your wife in that pickle?

SULLEN. What! not lie with my wife! why, sir, do you take me for an atheist or a rake?

SIR CHARLES. If you hate her, sir, I think you had better lie from her.

SULLEN. I think so too, friend – But I'm a Justice of Peace, and must do nothing against the law.

SIR CHARLES. Law! as I take it, Mr. Justice, no body observes law for law's sake, only for the good of those for whom it was made.

SULLEN. But if the law orders me to send you to gaol, you must lie there, my friend.

SIR CHARLES. Not unless I commit a crime to deserve it.

SULLEN. A crime! Oons an't I married?

SIR CHARLES. Nay, sir, if you call marriage a crime, you must disown it for a law.

SULLEN. Eh! – I must be acquainted with you, sir – But, sir, I should be very glad to know the truth of this matter.

SIR CHARLES. Truth, sir, is a profound sea, and few there be that dare wade deep enough to find out the bottom on't. Besides, sir, I'm afraid the line of your understanding mayn't be long enough.

SULLEN. Look'ee, sir, I have nothing to say to your sea of truth, but if a good parcel of land can entitle a man to a little truth, I have as much as any he in the country.

BONNIFACE. I never heard your Worship, as the saying is, talk so much before.

SULLEN. Because I never met with a man that I lik'd before –

BONNIFACE. Pray, sir, as the saying is, let me ask you one question, are not man and wife one flesh?

SIR CHARLES. You and your wife, Mr. Guts, may be one flesh, because ye are nothing else – but rational creatures have minds that must be united.

SULLEN. Minds.

SIR CHARLES. Ay, minds, sir, don't you think that the mind takes place of the body?

SULLEN. In some people.

SIR CHARLES. Then the interest of the master must be consulted before that of his servant.

SULLEN. Sir, you shall dine with me tomorrow. – Oons I always thought that we were naturally one.

SIR CHARLES. Sir, I know that my two hands are naturally one, because they love one another, kiss one another, help one another in all the actions of life, but I could not say so much, if they were always at cuffs.

SULLEN. Then 'tis plain that we are two.

SIR CHARLES. Why don't you part with her, sir?

SULLEN. Will you take her, sir?

SIR CHARLES. With all my heart.

SULLEN. You shall have her tomorrow morning, and a venison-pasty into the bargain.

SIR CHARLES. You'll let me have her fortune too?

SULLEN. Fortune! why, sir, I have no quarrel at her fortune – I only hate the woman, sir, and none but the woman shall go.

SIR CHARLES. But her fortune, sir –

SULLEN. Can you play at whisk, sir?

SIR CHARLES. No, truly, sir.

SULLEN. Nor at all-fours?

SIR CHARLES. Neither!

SULLEN. Oons! where was this man bred. (*Aside.*) Burn me, sir, I can't go home, 'tis but two a'clock.

SIR CHARLES. For half an hour, sir, if you please – But you must consider 'tis late.

SULLEN. Late! that's the reason I can't go to bed – Come, sir. –

Exeunt.

Enter CHERRY, *runs across the stage and knocks at* AIMWELL's *chamber door. Enter* AIMWELL *in his night-cap and gown.*

AIMWELL. What's the matter, you tremble, child, you're frighted.

CHERRY. No wonder, sir – But in short, sir, this very minute a gang of rogues are gone to rob my Lady Bountiful's house.

AIMWELL. How!

CHERRY. I dogg'd 'em to the very door, and left 'em breaking in.

AIMWELL. Have you alarm'd any body else with the news?

CHERRY. No, no, sir, I wanted to have discover'd the whole plot, and twenty other things to your man Martin; but I have search'd the whole house and can't find him; where is he?

AIMWELL. No matter, child, will you guide me immediately to the house?

CHERRY. With all my heart, sir, my Lady Bountiful is my god-mother; and I love Mrs. Dorinda so well –

AIMWELL. Dorinda! The name inspires me, the glory and the danger shall be all my own – Come, my life, let me but get my sword.

Exeunt.

[Act V, Scene ii]

Scene changes to a bed-chamber in Lady Bountiful's house. Enter MRS
SULLEN. DORINDA *undress'd, a table and lights.*

DORINDA. 'Tis very late, sister, no news of your spouse yet?

MRS SULLEN. No, I'm condemn'd to be alone till towards four,
   and then perhaps I may be executed with his company.

DORINDA. Well, my dear, I'll leave you to your rest; you'll go
   directly to bed, I suppose.

MRS SULLEN. I don't know what to do? hey-ho.

DORINDA. That's a desiring sigh, sister.

MRS SULLEN. This is a languishing hour, sister.

DORINDA. And might prove a critical minute, if the pretty fellow
   were here.

MRS SULLEN. Here! what, in my bed-chamber, at two a'clock
   o'th' morning, I undress'd, the family asleep, my hated husband
   abroad, and my lovely fellow at my feet – O gad, sister!

DORINDA. Thoughts are free, sister, and them I allow you – So,
   my dear, good night.

MRS SULLEN. A good rest to my dear Dorinda – Thoughts free!
   are they so? why then suppose him here, dress'd like a youthful,
   gay and burning bridegroom, (*Here* ARCHER *steals out of the closet.*)
   with tongue enchanting, eyes bewitching, knees imploring. (*Turns
   a little o' one side, and sees* ARCHER *in the posture she describes.*) Ah!
   (*Shrieks, and runs to the other side of the stage.*) Have my thoughts rais'd
   a spirit? – What are you, sir, a man or a Devil?

ARCHER. A man, a man, madam. (*Rising.*)

MRS SULLEN. How shall I be sure of it?

ARCHER. Madam, I'll give you demonstration this minute. (*Takes
   her hand.*)

MRS SULLEN. What, sir! do you intend to be rude?

ARCHER. Yes, madam, if you please.

MRS SULLEN. In the name of wonder, whence came ye?

ARCHER. From the skies, madam – I'm a Jupiter in love, and you shall be my Alcmena.

MRS SULLEN. How came you in?

ARCHER. I flew in at the window, madam, your cousin Cupid lent me his wings, and your sister Venus open'd the casement.

MRS SULLEN. I'm struck dumb with admiration.

ARCHER. And I with wonder.

Looks passionately at her.

MRS SULLEN. What will become of me?

ARCHER. How beautiful she looks – The teeming jolly spring smiles in her blooming face, and when she was conceiv'd, her mother smelt to roses, look'd on lilies –

Lilies unfold their white, their fragrant charms,
When the warm sun thus darts into their arms.

Runs to her.

MRS SULLEN. Ah! (*Shrieks.*)

ARCHER. Oons, madam, what d'ye mean? you'll raise the house.

MRS SULLEN. Sir, I'll wake the dead before I bear this – What! approach me with the freedoms of a keeper; I'm glad on't, your impudence has cur'd me.

ARCHER. If this be impudence (*Kneels.*) I leave to your partial self; no panting pilgrim after a tedious, painful voyage, e'er bow'd before his saint with more devotion.

MRS SULLEN. Now, now, I'm ruin'd, if he kneels! (*Aside.*) Rise thou prostrate engineer, not all thy undermining skill shall reach my heart – rise, and know, I am a woman without my sex, I can love to all the tenderness of wishes, sighs and tears – But go no farther – Still to convince you that I'm more than woman, I can speak my frailty, confess my weakness even for you – But –

ARCHER. For me!

Going to lay hold on her.

MRS SULLEN. Hold, sir, build not upon that – For my most mortal hatred follows if you disobey what I command you now – leave me this minute – If he denies, I'm lost. (*Aside.*)

ARCHER. Then you'll promise –

MRS SULLEN. Any thing another time.

ARCHER. When shall I come?

MRS SULLEN. Tomorrow when you will.

ARCHER. Your lips must seal the promise.

MRS SULLEN. Pshaw!

ARCHER. They must, they must – (*Kisses her.*) Raptures and paradise! and why not now, my angel? the time, the place, silence and secrecy, all conspire – And the now conscious stars have preordain'd this moment for my happiness.

Takes her in his arms.

MRS SULLEN. You will not, cannot sure.

ARCHER. If the sun rides fast, and disappoints not mortals of tomorrow's dawn, this night shall crown my joys.

MRS SULLEN. My sex's pride assist me.

ARCHER. My sex's strength help me.

MRS SULLEN. You shall kill me first.

ARCHER. I'll die with you.

Carrying her off.

MRS SULLEN. Thieves, thieves, murther —

Enter SCRUB in his breeches, and one shoe.

SCRUB. Thieves, thieves, murther, popery.

ARCHER. Ha! the very timorous stag will kill in rutting time.

Draws and offers to stab SCRUB.

SCRUB (*kneeling*). O, pray, sir, spare all I have and take my life.

MRS SULLEN (*holding* ARCHER'*s hand*). What do's the fellow mean?

SCRUB. O, madam, down upon your knees, your marrow-bones – He's one of 'um.

ARCHER. Of whom?

SCRUB. One of the rogues – I beg your pardon, sir, one of the honest gentlemen that just now are broke into the house.

ARCHER. How!

MRS SULLEN. I hope, you did not come to rob me?

ARCHER. Indeed I did, madam, but I would have taken nothing but what you might ha' spar'd, but your crying thieves has wak'd this dreaming fool, and so he takes 'em for granted.

SCRUB. Granted! 'tis granted, sir, take all we have.

MRS SULLEN. The fellow looks as if he were broke out of Bedlam.

SCRUB. Oons, madam, they're broke in to the house with fire and sword, I saw them, heard them, they'll be here this minute.

ARCHER. What, thieves!

SCRUB. Under favour, sir, I think so.

MRS SULLEN. What shall we do, sir?

ARCHER. Madam, I wish your Ladyship a good night.

MRS SULLEN. Will you leave me?

ARCHER. Leave you! Lord, madam, did not you command me to be gone just now upon pain of your immortal hatred.

MRS SULLEN. Nay, but pray, sir –

Takes hold of him.

ARCHER. Ha, ha, ha, now comes my turn to be ravish'd. – You see now, madam, you must use men one way or other; but take this by the way, good madam, that none but a fool will give you the benefit of his courage, unless you'll take his love along with it. – How are they arm'd, friend?

SCRUB. With sword and pistol, sir.

ARCHER. Hush – I see a dark lanthorn coming through the gallery. – Madam, be assur'd I will protect you, or lose my life.

MRS SULLEN. Your life! no, sir, they can rob me of nothing that I value half so much; therefore, now, sir, let me entreat you to be gone.

ARCHER. No, madam, I'll consult my own safety for the sake of yours, I'll work by stratagem: Have you courage enough to stand the appearance of 'em?

MRS SULLEN. Yes, yes, since I have scap'd your hands, I can face any thing.

ARCHER. Come hither, brother Scrub, don't you know me?

SCRUB. Eh! my dear brother, let me kiss thee.

Kisses ARCHER.

ARCHER. This way – Here –

ARCHER *and* SCRUB *hide behind the bed. Enter* GIBBET *with a dark lanthorn in one hand and a pistol in t'other.*

GIBBET. Ay, ay, this is the chamber, and the lady alone.

MRS SULLEN. Who are you, sir? what would you have? d'ye come to rob me?

GIBBET. Rob you! alack a day, madam, I'm only a younger brother, madam; and so, madam, if you make a noise, I'll shoot you through the head; but don't be afraid, madam.

Laying his lanthorn and pistol upon the table.

These rings, madam, don't be concern'd, madam, I have a profound respect for you, madam; your keys, madam, don't be frighted, madam, I'm the most of a gentleman.

Searching her pockets.

This necklace, madam, I never was rude to a lady; – I have a veneration – for this necklace –

Here ARCHER *having come round and seiz'd the pistols, takes* GIBBET *by the collar, trips up his heels, and claps the pistol to his breast.*

ARCHER. Hold, profane villain, and take the reward of thy sacrilege.

GIBBET. Oh! pray, sir, don't kill me; I an't prepar'd.

ARCHER. How many is there of 'em, Scrub?

SCRUB. Five and forty, sir.

ARCHER. Then I must kill the villain to have him out of the way.

GIBBET. Hold, hold, sir, we are but three upon my honour.

ARCHER. Scrub, will you undertake to secure him?

SCRUB. Not I, sir; kill him, kill him.

ARCHER. Run to Gipsey's chamber, there you'll find the Doctor; bring him hither presently.

Exit SCRUB *running.*

Come, rogue, if you have a short prayer, say it.

GIBBET. Sir, I have no prayer at all; the government has provided a chaplain to say prayers for us on these occasions.

MRS SULLEN. Pray, sir, don't kill him; – You fright me as much as him.

ARCHER. The dog shall die, madam, for being the occasion of my disappointment. – sirrah, this moment is your last.

GIBBET. Sir, I'll give you two hundred pound to spare my life.

ARCHER. Have you no more, rascal?

GIBBET. Yes, sir, I can command four hundred; but I must rescue two of 'em to save my life at the Sessions.

Enter SCRUB *and* FOIGARD.

ARCHER. Here, Doctor, I suppose Scrub and you between you may manage him. – Lay hold of him, Doctor.

FOIGARD *lays hold of* GIBBET.

GIBBET. What! turn'd over to the priest already. – Look'ye, Doctor, you come before your time; I an't condemn'd yet, I thank'ye.

FOIGARD. Come, my dear joy, I vill secure your body and your shoul too; I vill make you a good Catholic, and give you an absolution.

GIBBET. Absolution! can you procure me a pardon, Doctor?

FOIGARD. No, joy. –

GIBBET. Then you and your absolution may go to the Devil.

ARCHER. Convey him into the cellar, there bind him: – Take the pistol, and if he offers to resist, shoot him through the head, – and come back to us with all the speed you can.

SCRUB. Ay, ay, come, Doctor, do you hold him fast, and I'll guard him.

MRS SULLEN. But how came the Doctor?

ARCHER. In short, madam –

Shrieking without.

S'death! the rogues are at work with the other ladies. – I'm vex'd I parted with the pistol; but I must fly to their assistance. – Will you stay here, madam, or venture your self with me.

MRS SULLEN. O, with you, dear sir, with you.

Takes him by the arm and exeunt.

[Act V, Scene iii]

Scene changes to another apartment in the same house. Enter HOUNSLOW *dragging in* LADY BOUNTIFUL, *and* BAGSHOT *hauling in* DORINDA; *the rogues with swords drawn.*

HOUNSLOW. Come, come, your jewels, Mistriss.

BAGSHOT. Your keys, your keys, old gentlewoman.

Enter AIMWELL *and* CHERRY.

AIMWELL. Turn this way, villains; I durst engage an army in such a cause.

He engages 'em both.

DORINDA. O, Madam, had I but a sword to help the brave man?

LADY BOUNTIFUL. There's three or four hanging up in the hall; but they won't draw. I'll go fetch one however.

Exit.

Enter ARCHER *and* MRS SULLEN.

ARCHER. Hold, hold, my Lord, every man his bird, pray.

They engage man to man, the rogues are thrown and disarm'd.

CHERRY. What! the rogues taken! then they'll impeach my father; I must give him timely notice.

Runs out.

ARCHER. Shall we kill the rogues?

AIMWELL. No, no, we'll bind them.

ARCHER. Ay, ay; here, madam, lend me your garter? (*To* MRS SULLEN *who stands by him.*)

MRS SULLEN. The Devil's in this fellow; he fights, loves, and banters, all in a breath. – Here's a cord that the rogues brought with 'em, I suppose.

ARCHER. Right, right, the rogue's destiny, a rope to hang himself. – Come, my Lord, this is but a scandalous sort of an

office, (*Binding the rogues together.*) if our adventures should end
in this sort of hangmanwork; but I hope there is something in
prospect that –

Enter SCRUB.

Well, Scrub, have you secur'd your tartar?

SCRUB. Yes, sir, I left the priest and him disputing about religion.

AIMWELL. And pray carry these gentlemen to reap the benefit of
the controversy.

Delivers the prisoners to SCRUB, *who leads 'em out.*

MRS SULLEN. Pray, sister, how came my Lord here?

DORINDA. And pray, how came the gentleman here?

MRS SULLEN. I'll tell you the greatest piece of villainy –

They talk in dumb show.

AIMWELL. I fancy, Archer, you have been more successful in your
adventures than the house-breakers.

ARCHER. No matter for my adventure, yours is the principal. –
Press her this minute to marry you, – now while she's hurried
between the palpitation of her fear, and the joy of her deliverance, now while the tide of her spirits are at high-flood –
Throw yourself at her feet; speak some romantic nonsense or
other; – Address her like Alexander in the height of his victory,
confound her senses, bear down her reason, and away with
her – The priest is now in the cellar, and dare not refuse to do
the work.

Enter LADY BOUNTIFUL.

AIMWELL. But how shall I get off without being observ'd?

ARCHER. You a lover! and not find a way to get off – Let me see.

AIMWELL. You bleed, Archer.

ARCHER. S'death, I'm glad on't; this wound will do the business –
I'll amuse the old lady and Mrs. Sullen about dressing my wound,
while you carry off Dorinda.

LADY BOUNTIFUL. Gentlemen, could we understand how you would be gratified for the services –

ARCHER. Come, come, my Lady, this is no time for compliments, I'm wounded, madam.

LADY BOUNTIFUL [and] MRS SULLEN. How! wounded!

DORINDA. I hope, sir, you have receiv'd no hurt?

AIMWELL. None but what you may cure.

Makes love in dumb show.

LADY BOUNTIFUL. Let me see your arm, sir. I must have some powder-sugar to stop the blood – O me! an ugly gash – upon my word, sir, you must go into bed.

ARCHER. Ay, my Lady a bed would do very well. – Madam, (*To* MRS. SULLEN.) – will you do me the favour to conduct me to a chamber?

LADY BOUNTIFUL. Do, do, daughter – while I get the lint and the probe and the plaister ready.

Runs out one way, AIMWELL *carries off* DORINDA *another.*

ARCHER. Come, madam, why don't you obey your mother's commands?

MRS SULLEN. How can you, after what is past, have the confidence to ask me?

ARCHER. And if you go to that, how can you after what is past, have the confidence to deny me? – Was not this blood shed in your defence, and my life expos'd for your protection. – Look'ye, madam, I'm none of your romantic fools, that fight giants and monsters for nothing; my valour is downright Swiss; I'm a soldier of fortune and must be paid.

MRS SULLEN. 'Tis ungenerous in you, sir, to upbraid me with your services.

ARCHER. 'Tis ungenerous in you, madam, not to reward 'em.

MRS SULLEN. How! at the expense of my honour.

ARCHER. Honour! can honour consist with ingratitude? if you
would deal like a woman of honour, do like a man of honour,
d'ye think I would deny you in such a case?

Enter a SERVANT.

SERVANT. Madam, my lady order'd me to tell you that your
brother is below at the gate?

MRS SULLEN. My brother? Heavens be prais'd. – Sir, he shall
thank you for your services, he has it in his power.

ARCHER. Who is your brother, madam?

MRS SULLEN. Sir Charles Freeman. – You'll excuse me, sir;
I must go and receive him.

ARCHER. Sir Charles Freeman! S'death and Hell! – My old
acquaintance. Now unless Aimwell has made good use of his
time, all our fair machine goes souse into the sea like the
Edistone.

Exit.

[Act V, Scene iv]

Scene changes to the gallery in the same house. Enter AIMWELL *and*
DORINDA.

DORINDA. Well, well, my Lord, you have conquer'd; your late
generous action will I hope, plead for my easy yielding, tho'
I must own your Lordship had a friend in the fort before.

AIMWELL. The sweets of Hybla dwell upon her tongue. – Here,
Doctor –

Enter FOIGARD *with a book.*

FOIGARD. Are you prepar'd boat?

DORINDA. I'm ready: But, first, my Lord one word; I have a
frightful example of a hasty marriage in my own family; when
I reflect upon't, it shocks me. Pray, my Lord, consider a little –

AIMWELL. Consider! Do you doubt my honour or my love?

DORINDA. Neither: I do believe you equally just as brave. – And
were your whole sex drawn out for me to choose, I should not
cast a look upon the multitude if you were absent. – But my Lord,
I'm a woman; Colours, concealments may hide a thousand faults
in me; – Therefore know me better first; I hardly dare affirm I
know my self in any thing except my love.

AIMWELL. Such goodness who could injure; I find my self unequal
to the task of villain; she has gain'd my soul, and made it honest
like her own; cannot, cannot hurt her. (*Aside.*) Doctor, retire.

Exit FOIGARD.

Madam, behold your lover and your proselyte, and judge of my
passion by my conversion. – I'm all a lie, nor dare I give a fiction
to your arms; I'm all counterfeit except my passion.

DORINDA. Forbid it heaven! a counterfeit!

AIMWELL. I am no Lord, but a poor needy man, come with a
mean, a scandalous design to prey upon your fortune: – But the
beauties of your mind and person have so won me from my self,
that like a trusty servant, I prefer the interest of my mistress to
my own.

DORINDA. Sure I have had the dream of some poor mariner, a
sleepy image of a welcome port, and wake involv'd in storms. –
Pray, sir, who are you?

AIMWELL. Brother to the man whose title I usurp'd, but stranger
to his honour or his fortune.

DORINDA. Matchless honesty – Once I was proud, sir, of your
wealth and title, but now am prouder that you want it: Now
I can show my love was justly levell'd, and had no aim but love.
Doctor, come in.

Enter FOIGARD *at one door,* GIPSEY *at another, who whispers* DORINDA.

Your pardon, sir, we shannot; won't you now, sir? you must excuse me, – I'll wait on you presently.

Exit with GIPSEY.

FOIGARD. Upon my shoul, now, dis is foolish.

Exit.

AIMWELL. Gone! and bid the priest depart. – It has an ominous look.

Enter ARCHER.

ARCHER. Courage, Tom – Shall I wish you joy?

AIMWELL. No.

ARCHER. Oons, man, what ha' you been doing?

AIMWELL. O, Archer, my honesty, I fear has ruin'd me.

ARCHER. How!

AIMWELL. I have discover'd myself.

ARCHER. Discover'd! and without my consent? what! have I embark'd my small remains in the same bottom with yours, and you dispose of all without my partnership?

AIMWELL. O, Archer, I own my fault.

ARCHER. After conviction – 'Tis then too late for pardon. – You may remember, Mr. Aimwell, that you propos'd this folly – As you begun, so end it. – Henceforth I'll hunt my fortune single. – So farewell.

AIMWELL. Stay, my dear Archer, but a minute.

ARCHER. Stay! what to be despis'd, expos'd and laugh'd at – No, I would sooner change conditions with the worst of the rogues we just now bound, than bear one scornful smile from the proud knight that once I treated as my equal.

AIMWELL. What knight?

ARCHER. Sir Charles Freeman, brother to the lady that I had almost – But no matter for that, 'tis a cursed night's work, and so I leave you to make your best on't.

Going.

AIMWELL. Freeman I – One word, Archer. Still I have hopes; methought she receiv'd my confession with pleasure.

ARCHER. S'death! who doubts it?

AIMWELL. She consented after to the match; and still I dare believe she will be just.

ARCHER. To herself, I warrant her, as you should have been.

AIMWELL. By all my hopes, she comes, and smiling comes.

Enter DORINDA *mighty gay.*

DORINDA. Come, my dear Lord, – I fly with impatience to your arms. – The minutes of my absence was a tedious year. Where's this tedious priest?

Enter FOIGARD.

ARCHER. Oons! a brave girl.

DORINDA. I suppose, my Lord, this gentleman is privy to our affairs?

ARCHER. Yes, yes, madam, I'm to be your father.

DORINDA. Come, priest, do your office.

ARCHER. Make haste, make haste, couple 'em any way.

Takes AIMWELL'*s hand.*

Come, madam, I'm to give you –

DORINDA. My mind's alter'd, I won't.

ARCHER. Eh –

AIMWELL. I'm confounded.

FOIGARD. Upon my shoul, and sho is my shelf.

ARCHER. What's the matter now, madam?

DORINDA. Look'ye, sir, one generous action deserves another –
This gentleman's honour oblig'd him to hide nothing from me;
my justice engages me to conceal nothing from him: In short, sir,
you are the person that you thought you counterfeited; you are
the true Lord Viscount Aimwell; and I wish your Lordship joy.
Now, priest, you may be gone; if my Lord is pleas'd now with the
match, let his Lordship marry me in the face of the world.

AIMWELL [and] ARCHER. What do's she mean?

DORINDA. Here's a witness for my truth.

Enter SIR CHARLES *and* MRS SULLEN.

SIR CHARLES. My dear Lord Aimwell, I wish you joy.

AIMWELL. Of what?

SIR CHARLES. Of your honour and estate: Your brother died the
day before I left London; and all your friends have writ after you
to Brussels; among the rest I did my self the honour.

ARCHER. Hark'ye, Sir Knight, don't you banter now?

SIR CHARLES. 'Tis truth upon my honour.

AIMWELL. Thanks to the pregnant stars that form'd this accident.

ARCHER. Thanks to the womb of time that brought it forth; away
with it.

AIMWELL. Thanks to my guardian angel that led me to the prize –

Taking DORINDA'*s hand.*

ARCHER. And double thanks to the noble Sir Charles Freeman.
My Lord, I wish you joy. My lady I wish you joy. – I'gad, Sir
Freeman, you're the honestest fellow living. – S'death, I'm grown
strange airy upon this matter – My Lord, how d'ye? – a word, my
Lord; don't you remember something of a previous agreement,
that entitles me to the moiety of this lady's fortune, which, I think
will amount to five thousand pound.

AIMWELL. Not a penny, Archer; You would ha' cut my throat just now, because I would not deceive this lady.

ARCHER. Ay, and I'll cut your throat again, if you should deceive her now.

AIMWELL. That's what I expected; and to end the dispute, the lady's fortune is ten thousand pound; we'll divide stakes; take the ten thousand pound, or the lady.

DORINDA. How! is your Lordship so indifferent?

ARCHER. No, no, no, madam, his Lordship knows very well, that I'll take the money; I leave you to his Lordship, and so we're both provided for.

Enter COUNT BELLAIR.

COUNT. *Mesdames, et Massieurs*, I am your servant trice humble: I hear you be rob, here.

AIMWELL. The ladies have been in some danger, sir.

COUNT. And begar, our inn be rob too.

AIMWELL. Our inn! by whom?

COUNT. By the landlord, begar – garzoon he has rob himself and run away.

ARCHER. Rob'd himself!

COUNT. Ay, begar, and me too of a hundred pound.

ARCHER. A hundred pound.

COUNT. Yes, that I ow'd him.

AIMWELL. Our money's gone, Frank.

ARCHER. Rot the money, my wench is gone – *Scavez vous quelque chose de Madamoiselle Cherry?*

Enter a FELLOW *with a strong box and a letter.*

FELLOW. Is there one Martin here?

ARCHER. Ay, ay, – who wants him?

FELLOW. I have a box here and letter for him.

ARCHER (*taking the box*). Ha, ha, ha, what's here? *Legerdemain!* by this light, my Lord, our money again; but this unfolds the riddle.

Opening the letter, reads.

Hum, hum, hum – O, 'tis for the public good, and must be communicated to the company.

Mr. MARTIN, *my father being afraid of an impeachment by the rogues that are taken tonight is gone off; but if you can procure him a pardon he will make great discoveries that may be useful to the country; could I have met you instead of your master tonight, I would have deliver'd myself into your hands with a sum that much exceeds that in your strong box, which I have sent you, with an assurance to my dear Martin, that I shall ever be his most faithful friend till death.*

CHERRY BONNIFACE.

There's a billet-doux for you – As for the father I think he ought to be encouraged, and for the daughter, – Pray, my Lord, persuade your bride to take her into her service instead of Gipsey.

AIMWELL. I can assure you, madam, your deliverance was owing to her discovery.

DORINDA. Your command, my Lord, will do without the obligation. I'll take care of her.

SIR CHARLES. This good company meets opportunely in favour of a design I have in behalf of my unfortunate sister, I intend to part her from her husband – Gentlemen will you assist me?

ARCHER. Assist you! S'death, who would not.

COUNT. Assist! Garzoon, we all assest.

Enter SULLEN.

SULLEN. What's all this? – They tell me spouse that you had like to have been robb'd.

MRS SULLEN. Truly, spouse, I was pretty near it – Had not these two gentlemen interpos'd.

SULLEN. How came these gentlemen here?

MRS SULLEN. That's his way of returning thanks you must know.

COUNT. Garzoon, the question be a propo for all dat.

SIR CHARLES. You promis'd last night, sir, that you would deliver your lady to me this morning.

SULLEN. Humph.

ARCHER. Humph. What do you mean by humph – Sir, you shall deliver her – In short, sir, we have sav'd you and your family, and if you are not civil we'll unbind the rogues, join with 'um and set fire to your house – What do's the man mean? not part with his wife!

COUNT. Ay, garzoon de man no understan common justice.

MRS SULLEN. Hold, gentlemen, all things here must move by consent, compulsion would spoil us, let my dear and I talk the matter over, and you shall judge it between us.

SULLEN. Let me know first who are to be our judges – Pray, sir, who are you?

SIR CHARLES. I am Sir Charles Freeman, come to take away your wife.

SULLEN. And you, good sir?

AIMWELL. Charles Viscount Aimwell, come to take away your sister.

SULLEN. And you pray, sir?

ARCHER. Francis Archer, Esq; come –

SULLEN. To take away my mother, I hope – gentlemen, you're heartily welcome, I never met with three more obliging people since I was born – And now, my dear, if you please, you shall have the first word.

ARCHER. And the last for five pound.

MRS SULLEN. Spouse.

SULLEN. Rib.

MRS SULLEN. How long have we been married?

SULLEN. By the almanack fourteen months – But by my account fourteen years.

MRS SULLEN. 'Tis thereabout by my reckoning.

COUNT. Garzoon, their account will agree.

MRS SULLEN. Pray, spouse, what did you marry for?

SULLEN. To get an heir to my estate.

SIR CHARLES. And have you succeeded?

SULLEN. No.

ARCHER. The condition fails of his side – Pray, madam, what did you marry for?

MRS SULLEN. To support the weakness of my sex by the strength of his, and to enjoy the pleasures of an agreeable society.

SIR CHARLES. Are your expectations answer'd?

MRS SULLEN. No.

COUNT. A clear case, a clear case.

SIR CHARLES. What are the bars to your mutual contentment.

MRS SULLEN. In the first place I can't drink ale with him.

SULLEN. Nor can I drink tea with her.

MRS SULLEN. I can't hunt with you.

SULLEN. Nor can I dance with you.

MRS SULLEN. I hate cocking and racing.

SULLEN. And I abhor ombre and piquet.

MRS SULLEN. Your silence is intolerable.

SULLEN. Your prating is worse.

MRS SULLEN. Have we not been a perpetual offence to each other – A gnawing vulture at the heart.

SULLEN. A frightful goblin to the sight.

MRS SULLEN. A porcupine to the feeling.

SULLEN. Perpetual wormwood to the taste.

MRS SULLEN. Is there on Earth a thing we could agree in?

SULLEN. Yes – to part.

MRS SULLEN. With all my heart.

SULLEN. Your hand.

MRS SULLEN. Here.

SULLEN. These hands join'd us, these shall part us – away –

MRS SULLEN. North.

SULLEN. South.

MRS SULLEN. East.

SULLEN. West – far as the poles asunder.

COUNT. Begar the ceremony be vera pretty.

SIR CHARLES. Now, Mr. Sullen, there wants only my sister's fortune to make us easy.

SULLEN. Sir Charles, you love your sister, and I love her fortune; every one to his fancy.

ARCHER. Then you won't refund?

SULLEN. Not a stiver.

ARCHER. Then I find, madam, you must e'en go to your prison again.

COUNT. What is the portion.

SIR CHARLES. Ten thousand pound, sir.

COUNT. Garzoon, I'll pay it, and she shall go home wid me.

ARCHER. Ha, ha, ha, French all over – Do you know, sir, what ten thousand pound English is?

COUNT. No, begar, not justement.

ARCHER. Why, sir, 'tis a hundred thousand livres.

COUNT. A hundre tousand livres – A garzoon, me canno' do't, your beauties and their fortunes are both too much for me.

ARCHER. Then I will – This night's adventure has prov'd strangely lucky to us all – For Captain Gibbet in his walk had made bold, Mr. Sullen, with your study and escritore, and had taken out all the writings of your estate, all the articles of marriage with his lady, bills, bonds, leases, receipts to an infinite value, I took 'em from him, and I deliver them to Sir Charles.

Gives him a parcel of papers and parchments.

SULLEN. How, my writings! my head aches consumedly – Well, gentlemen, you shall have her fortune, but I can't talk. If you have a mind, Sir Charles, to be merry, and celebrate my sister's wedding, and my divorce, you may command my house – but my head aches consumedly – Scrub, bring me a dram.

ARCHER. Madam, (*To* MRS. SULLEN.) there's a country dance to the trifle that I sung today; your hand, and we'll lead it up.

Here a dance.

ARCHER. 'Twould be hard to guess which of these parties is the better pleas'd, the couple joined, or the couple parted? the one rejoicing in hopes of an untasted happiness, and the other in their deliverance from an experienc'd misery.

Both happy in their several states we find,
Those parted by consent, and those conjoin'd.
Consent, if mutual, saves the lawyer's fee,
Consent is law enough to set you free.

Finis.

An Epilogue

Design'd to be spoke in the Beaux Stratagem.

If to our play your judgment can't be kind,
Let its expiring author pity find.
Survey his mournful case with melting eyes,
Nor let the bard be damn'd before he dies.
Forbear you fair on his last scene to frown,
But his true exit with a plaudit crown;
Then shall the dying poet cease to fear,
The dreadful knell, while your applause he hears.
At Leuctra so, the conqu'ring Theban died,
Claim'd his friend's praises, but their tears denied:
Pleas'd in the pangs of death he greatly thought
Conquest with loss of life but cheaply bought.
The difference this, the Greek was one would fight
As brave, tho' not so gay as Sergeant Kite;
Ye sons of Will's what's that to those who write ?
To Thebes alone the Grecian ow'd his bays,
You may the bard above the hero raise,
Since yours is greater than Athenian praise.

Glossary

Acts of a play, steal two – That is, avoid payment for a side box, since this was not demanded till the end of the second act. The context seems to suggest that successive acts of the same play have been seen on a single day's outing, one at each of the licensed theatres. For this the opportunity would have been most infrequent.

Airy – Gay, flippant.

Alcmena – Mother of Hercules. The night of his conception was said to have been extended to three times its proper length at the command of Zeus, for his mistress's better pleasure.

All-fours – A card game for two.

Amadis – The eponymous hero of the *Amadis de Gaul*, a Spanish romance of the fourteenth century.

Bays – The victor's (or the laureate's) crowning wreath of bay leaves.

Blazing star – Comet.

Bohee – A kind of black tea.

Brentford, old – A 'town of mud' (Thomson's *The Castle of Indolence*).

Bully – A protector of prostitutes.

Cedunt arma togae – 'The sword gives way to the gown.'

Cephalic plaster – A plaster not for the feet, but the head.

Cereuse – A cosmetic for whitening the skin.

Cesario – Viola's male *alter ego* in Shakespeare's *Twelfth Night*.

Chin-cough – Whooping cough.

Club o'th'reckoning, pay our – Contribute to the pool of money for settling the account.

Counterscarp – The outer wall of a fortified ditch.

Demi-cannons – One of the larger kinds of cannon, weighing some six thousand pounds.

Dings about – Sets upon those around her.

Doctors-Commons – The College of Civil Law which then dealt in marriage settlements, divorces and wills.

Edistone – The first, wooden Eddystone Lighthouse was completed in 1699, but destroyed in a storm on 27 November 1703.

Engineer – Plotter.

Escritore – Private writing-desk.

Execution in, do – Impress your personal distinctions upon.

Expiring author – Wilks perpetuated the tradition that Farquhar died on 13 March 1707, the third night of *The Beaux Stratagem*. In fact he was buried (at Wilks's expense) on 23 May.

Fat ale – Full-bodied, strong ale.

Fits of the mother – Hysteria.

Gallows-foot, beg that fellow at the – That is, save him from hanging by an offer of marriage at the scaffold.

Gold keys – The insignia of the Lord Chamberlain.

Grace, his – Assumed to be a casual hit at His Grace the Duke of Ormond, who had let Farquhar down after promising to obtain him a commission.

Green sickness – A kind of anaemia, most prevalent among young girls during puberty.

Half seas over – Drunk.

Hungary-water – A perfume compounded of rosemary flowers and spirit.

Kings-evil – Scrofula.

Kite – The wily sergeant in Farquhar's previous play, *The Recruiting Officer*.

Lay, put it upon that – Take that risk.

Le Brun . . . Arbela – The French artist Le Brun was commissioned by Louis XIV to depict the battles of Alexander the Great. Archer is contrasting battles fought under the Duke of Marlborough with those of Alexander.

Leuctra – The Thebans defeated the Spartans at Leuctra in 371 BC. But it was at the battle at Mantinea in 362 BC that the Theban leader, Epaminondas, died in the moment of his victory.

Levee – Reception for a great man's petitioners and sycophants.

Lion and the Rose – Rooms in the inn, at that date known by names.

Morris – A coffee-house keeper.

Mountebank – Charlatan, confidence-trickster.

Old style – According to the Julian calendar: the Gregorian was not introduced into England until 1752.

Originals – That is, in the additional sense of eccentric or unique characters.

Oroondates – A character in La Calprenède's *Cassandra*, first translated in 1652.

Parliament man – Member of Parliament. Cherry assumes that Aimwell's money is to be used for purchasing votes.

Phillis has her Coridon, every – Allusively, every pastoral lover has his or her mate.

Plain-Dealer – William Wycherley, whose play of that name was first performed in 1674.

Premisses – That is, the articles previously enumerated. A legal phrase, used ironically.

Pressing Act – The Mutiny and Impressment Acts of 1703-05 enabled magistrates to levy all those 'who have not any lawful calling or employment . . . to serve as soldiers'.

Proselyte – A convert; one now won over to a cause.

Quoif – A tightly-fitting white cap.

Roman – In military jargon, a foot-soldier ready to fight for his country without payment.

Simony – A means of purchasing ecclesiastical preferment: hence, here, a bribe to secure a good pew.

Simpling – Gathering: originally, searching for 'simples' or medicinal herbs.

Sir Simon the King – A popular tune included in Playford's *Musick's Recreation* in 1652, and believed to celebrate the memory of Simon Wardloe, landlord of the Devil Tavern off Fleet Street in the early seventeenth century.

Spain, what King of – Foigard is being asked to declare his allegiance in the War of the Spanish Succession, between Philip, grandson of Louis XIV, and the Archduke Charles of Austria.

Stiver – A Dutch coin, roughly equivalent to a penny.

Swiss – Mercenary.

Tapis, upon the – Under discussion (upon the tapestried council table).

Teague – Then the commonest colloquialism for an Irishman.

Toftida – Katherine Tofts, the native-born prima-donna then at the height of her fame. She retired from the stage in 1709.

Trifle, to the – That is, as an accompaniment to the song assigned to Archer in the third act.

Tun – A cask equivalent to four hogsheads, containing about 200 gallons of ale.

Tympanies – Swellings.

Union – That is, the Union of the English and Scottish Parliaments, enacted on 6 March 1707, two days before the first performance of *The Beaux Stratagem*.

Usquebaugh – Whisky.

Vigo business – An affair as profitable as Sir George Rook's action off Vigo in October 1702.

Weekly bills – That is, within the central districts of London for which weekly bills of mortality and of its various causes were issued.

Whisk – Whist.

White rods – Carried by both the Lord Chamberlain and the Lord High Treasurer as marks of office.

Willing tits – Sound horses.

Will's – A coffee house in Bow Street, famous for its literary clientele.